The Lord with Us

From the Book of Hebrews

From the Book of Hebrews
The Lord with Us

Tim R. Barker, D. Min.

Superintendent of the South Texas District of the Assemblies of God

Tim R. Barker Ministries

THE LORD WITH US: FROM THE BOOK OF HEBREWS, Barker, Tim.

1st ed.

Scripture passages are from The Holy Bible, New International Version® (NIV®), copyright © 1973, 1978, 1984, 2011 by Biblica, Inc.™ All rights reserved. Used by permission of Zondervan.

This book and its contents are wholly the creation and intellectual property of Tim Barker.

This book may not be reproduced in whole or in part, by electronic process or any other means, without written permission of the author.

ISBN: 978-1-7358529-1-1

Copyright © 2021 by Tim Barker

All Rights Reserved

Dedication

I want to dedicate this book to our nearly 1,000 South Texas Assemblies of God Ministers who have pastored the uncertainties associated with Covid-19! I'm constantly reminding myself, as well as others that God knew we'd be serving during this season of challenges. Through it all, we've felt THE LORD WITH US every step of the way!

Table of Contents

Rest in a Busy World............................	1
Obedience to the Word	6
Keeping Faith.....................................	15
Entering God's Presence.....................	30
Creating a Firm Foundation	52
Drawing Near to God	56
Lifting Up Others.................................	72
Godly Discipline..................................	81
Power in Thanksgiving!	104
Christ, the Only Way	112
More than Lip Service	121
About Tim R. Barker...........................	131

A Final Word 133

Rest in a Busy World

Hebrews 4:1-3

We live in an extremely busy world, even with all of the modern conveniences available. The word "rest" is almost missing from our vocabulary! People often talk about needing to get some "rest." The frantic lifestyle we live today has also affected our spiritual man. We get so busy that we can have frantic activity in preparation for ministry (spiritually) and fail to enter into God's rest! Israel experienced this in the wilderness, failing to rest and acknowledge God – and we do as well too many times.

The only way to enter God's rest is through faith in His Word and obedience to that Word – failure to obey God's Word will leave us unrested! We ultimately rest in the person of Jesus Christ who has finished the work of redemption for us, so that if we live in a true relationship with Jesus, "rest" is possible!

J. I. Packer said, "Certainty about the great issues of the Christian faith and conduct is lacking all along the line. The outside observer sees us staggering on from gimmick to gimmick and stunt to stunt like so many drunks in a fog, not knowing at all where we are or which way we should be going. Preaching is hazy; heads are muddled; hearts fret; doubts drain strength; uncertainty paralyzes action. Unlike the first Christians who in three centuries won the Roman world, and those later Christians who pioneered the Reformation, and the Puritan awakening and the Evangelical revival, and the great missionary movement of the last century, we lack certainty. Why is this? We blame the external pressures of modern secularism, but this is like Eve blaming the serpent. The truth is that we have grieved the Spirit ... we stand under divine judgment. For two generations our churches have suffered from a famine of hearing the words of the Lord." That's a tragic truth.

It's easy today to blame everything around us for our restlessness and losses, but it may be time that we examine the real reason for our lack of rest, our own avoidance of obedience to God's Word! The Bible teaches us that we can fail to enter God's rest if we fail to accept Christ's sacrifice for salvation and fail to obey His Word, that the lack of obedience is a lack of faith, which leads to a lack of rest!

Hebrews 4:3

Now we who have believed enter that rest, just as God has said, "So I declared on oath in my anger, 'They shall never enter my rest.'" And yet his work has been finished since the creation of the world.

God has always promised a "rest" to those who want it! Even in the Old Testament there was a rest in God that was possible. Unfortunately as the preceding verses indicate, Israel failed to find this "rest" of God's! How tragic that they missed the most important "rest" God had to offer. But this "rest" remains for anyone today who might want it!

It is not a physical rest that God is speaking of here, it is a spiritual rest! This promise has been available for a long time and will continue to be available until Jesus comes back again.

For those who want "rest," it is available, and the writer will describe here how we go about finding it. God's rest comes from faith in God's Word – which leads to obedience! Notice in Hebrews 3:19... *"So, we see that they (Israel) were not able to enter, because of their unbelief."* (Which led to their disobedience – there is a direct connection between REAL faith and obedience!)

William Bradford, the governor of the Plymouth Colony of pilgrims, insisted, "Those who believe in the Holy Scriptures are bound to observe its teachings. Those who do not are to be bound by its consequences."

The rewards are great; the consequences for failure to obey are also great!

Those who call themselves "Christians" but fail to live according to God's Word will not enter God's rest! Israel's sufferings were the result of their own disobedience and lack of faith in God's Word even though God was present in the very midst of their camp by the fire at night and the cloud by day! God's rest is available, but only through faith and obedience to His Word!

Obedience to the Word

Hebrews 4:4-13

The messages from God can be of no value if they are not received by faith and receiving them by faith implies obedience to that Word! Disobedience is a form of unbelief! The things we believe in we tend to express in real ways, so saying we believe in God WILL MEAN living out a life of obedience to God's Word ... if we truly believe it! This was Israel's constant problem in the desert, they heard God's Word through His servant Moses, but they did not have enough faith in it to obey it, hence the consequences that they never entered God's rest!

Israel loved the miracles and the displays of God's power, but they did not obey God's Word and thus they forfeited the most important rest God had to offer them! If they failed to enter God's rest even with God's presence in their midst and the miracles, SO CAN WE! They were reckless with God and their own lives; they failed to see that disobedience could lead to bad consequences later!

Howard Hendricks shared that if you've ever been to Yellowstone National Park, you were probably given a piece of paper by a ranger at the park entrance. On it in big letters was the warning *"Do Not Feed the Bears."* You no sooner drive into the heart of the park, however, than you see people feeding the bears. When he first saw this, he asked a ranger about it. "Sir," he answered, "you have only a small part of the picture." He described how the park service personnel in the fall and winter must carry away the bodies of dead bears – bears who have lost their ability to fend for food. That's what's happening to us.

Too many people who call themselves Christians today live this way! They are reckless with God's Word! They can raise hands in worship, or praise God for miracles, but they do not live in obedience to God's Word. In some cases they openly mock God's Word and its teachings! And then they wonder why their lives are anything but "rested" in God! We will not experience God's beautiful rest if it is in church only that we act like believers!

One cannot say they have faith in God without also having faith in His Word, and one cannot say he has faith in the Word of God if he is not willing to obey it! When we bypass God's Word it doesn't matter how we feel about God, we are living reckless lives! (Heb. 4:6) To ignore God's Word is to put your spiritual life in jeopardy. It won't matter how many verses of the Bible you know by heart, how many powerful experiences you had at the altar, or how intensely you can sing Gospel choruses, you will not find God's rest without obedience to His Word! This is what Israel's example teaches us here! They ran toward miracles, but away from God's Word and the result was that they self-destructed!

Several years ago, newspapers reported how a new Navy jet fighter shot itself down. Flying at supersonic speed, it ran into cannon shells it had fired only a few seconds before. The jet was traveling too fast! You are also traveling too fast, if you don't have time to worship God in regular church services, if you don't have time to read the Bible, if you don't have time to pray. If you're neglecting any of these, you're probably traveling too fast to hear the sound of God's voice. You can't tell whether you are in the center of His will. Better slow down before, like the jet, you shoot yourself down.

There are too many reckless people who call themselves "Christians" today in the church. We can make the same mistake as Israel did, hence the warning in Hebrews 4:11 is real!

Hebrews 4:11

Let us, therefore, make every effort to enter that rest, so that no one will perish by following their example of disobedience.

The language here is strange and ironic in a sense: *"Let us LABOR therefore to enter that rest."* (KJV) Ironic in the sense that we must *"make every effort"* (NIV) or *"labor"* (KJV) to enter this rest! The idea here means simply that we do have choices: to obey the Word of God by faith or disobey it through unbelief! Obedience to God's Word can bring us into God's rest; disobedience will leave us outside without rest! There must be more to our faith than knowing doctrine; we must live it!

It is simply not enough to just be willing to get saved but then not live by the Word of God!

The book, *A Long Obedience in the Same Direction* by Eugene H. Peterson, states, "It is not difficult in our world to get a person interested in the message of the Gospel; it is terrifically difficult to sustain the interest. Millions of people in our culture make decisions for Christ, but there is a dreadful attrition rate. Many claim to have been born again, but the evidence for mature Christian discipleship is slim. In our kind of culture anything, even news about God, can be sold if it is packaged freshly; but when it loses its novelty, it goes on the garbage heap. There is a great market for religious experience in our world; there is little enthusiasm for the patient acquisition of virtue, little inclination to sign up for a long apprenticeship in what earlier generations of Christians called holiness."

The Christian life does not consist in just the altar call experience, it is also the lifestyle of obedience to the Word of God by faith that matters! Too many people are willing to embrace Jesus so they can get to heaven, but they don't want to hear what the Bible teaches about their sinful lifestyle that requires changes! Obedience however is a requirement or there can be no rest for the wicked! It is this "LABORING" to obey God's Word that brings us into spiritual health and restfulness! This is a daily task. If we truly have faith in God's Word, we will follow it! Just as there are no shortcuts to good physical health, there can be none to good spiritual health!

According to a researcher at the University of Michigan, a program of good exercise may help a person fight off colds and infection. The theory is that a good workout puts the body in a condition similar to what happens at the onset of a fever. That's not all bad. Most biologists are of the opinion that a fever is the body's way of fighting back when micro intruders get into the system. Increased body temperature seems to aid the white-cell defense system while slowing down the action of bacteria and viruses. Exercise, it is now thought, does the same thing. It releases chemicals into the blood that stimulate the brain to make our temperature rise.

The Bible teaches that a regular course of good spiritual exercise is highly beneficial to the health of our soul. It shows us that sin is effectively warded off in a person who is walking in the light, one who is obeying Jesus each day. On the other hand, disobedience or following the path of least resistance cools down a person's spiritual temperature. Fellowship is neglected. Sin is neither confessed nor forsaken. The result is a lukewarm or cold Christian who is not taking advantage of the kind of defenses necessary to fight spiritual infection where it exists.

There were only Joshua and Caleb who had entered into God's rest, the only two to believe God's Word and obey it. The rest of that generation died in the wilderness having failed to ever enter God's rest although they had God's presence in their camp and His miracles on their journey! The only difference was obedience! Many times, this is still the only difference of why one Christian does well, and another is always struggling and void of rest! The "rested" one is actively serving God and living a life of obedience to the Word, while the one who feels spiritually "tired" all the time is the one who has neglected those same disciplines. This is God's requirement for His rest ... exercise the Word of God daily!

Hebrews 4:12-13

^{12} For the word of God is alive and active. Sharper than any double-edged sword, it penetrates even to dividing soul and spirit, joints, and marrow; it judges the thoughts and attitudes of the heart. ^{13} Nothing in all creation is hidden from God's sight. Everything is uncovered and laid bare before the eyes of him to whom we must give account.

Notice how this paragraph ends – with the Word of God again in the focus!

It is that Word of God that ultimately impacts the quality of our spiritual life in the here and now as well as the then and there! The Word of God is foundational to our spiritual health. It must have priority in our life, and this is done by obedience to its teachings! There is nothing else on earth that can do what the Word of God can do! It is alive and active; it can pierce through anything! All attempts to disregard God's Word will end up in failure, and we cannot hide our sins which is nothing more than disobedience to His Word! The Word of God has the power to change everything and only it brings rest!

How tragic that an entire generation wandered through a desert simply because they failed to enter into God's rest by faith and obedience to His Word! Yet, we could have an entire generation do the same thing today, or an individual! We must be people of the Word, not people of the World! If we are to really know God's rest in our souls, we must have faith in God and His Word and obey it! How rested are you?

Though Israel was called "God's people" and though they had seen miracles and God's great power, they failed to enter God's rest! Failure to enter was because of their failure to believe God's Word, which led to disobedience, with the result: NO REST! The same can happen today too. Obedience is the evidence of faith which leads to rest! How restful is your life?

Keeping Faith

Hebrews 4:14-16
Matthew 4:1-11

Starting off in faith is a good thing but staying in faith is a great thing! We need to be cautious that we don't lose a firm grip on our faith, for if we do, we will find ourselves really floundering with an unproductive spirituality.

There are two things that can help us hold firmly to the faith: Christ as our high priest understands our weaknesses and is sympathetic to helping us – we don't have to be alone! And Christ gives us His own example on how to fight the various kinds of temptations that Satan uses to draw us away from keeping our faith focused properly.

If there is one thing the Bible is clear about, it is

that faith has to be exercised in order for us to stay firm in it! This will certainly be the case as we come into the last days where the Bible states that many will be deceived, and even the elect of God must be careful that they are not deceived!

The one thing we can be sure of is that we will be tempted! If we yield, we will not have firm faith. We need to understand the *nature of HUMAN FLESH*, and the *nature of HOLY FAITH!*

The Bible teaches us that when we are tempted God is willing to help us, Christ faced temptation and beat it, and what He used is available to us today too – so, *"let us hold firmly to the faith!"*

Hebrews 4:14-15

[14] Therefore, since we have a great high priest who has ascended into heaven, Jesus the Son of God, let us hold firmly to the faith we profess. [15] For we do not have a high priest who is unable to empathize with our weaknesses, but we have one who has been tempted in every way, just as we are—yet he did not sin.

People quit when they feel they are alone and no one understands! No one likes the feeling that something can't succeed. No one likes facing something that seems overwhelming. So often we feel God doesn't understand the pressures we go through, that in His perfection He couldn't possibly know pain and loneliness. This is where the incarnation comes in! Jesus came in human flesh as God so that there would be a way for Him to "feel" and know our human weaknesses. God did not stay out of harm's way. He faced it squarely so He can help us through the storms of life and when we feel our faith is slipping!

I read the story of Joseph Mallord Turner, English painter, who invited Charles Kingsley to his studio to see a picture of a storm at sea. In rapt admiration, Kingsley exclaimed, "It's wonderful! It's so realistic! How did you do it?" The artist replied, "I went to the coast of Holland and engaged a fisherman to take me out to sea in the next storm. Entering his boat as a storm was brewing, I asked him to bind me to the mast. Then he steered his boat into the teeth of the storm. The storm raged with such fury that at times I longed to be in the bottom of the boat where the waves would blow over me. I could not, however. I was bound to the mast. Not only did I see the storm in its raging fury, but I also felt it! It blew into me, as it were, until I became a part of it. After this terrible ordeal, I returned to my studio and painted the picture."

Christ can understand completely our struggle and pain. He has experienced it all. He both shows us the way to hold on by His example as well as ministering to us because He also knows our human frame! Christ sympathizes with our struggle, and He conquered using the same tool available to us, God's Word!

Hebrews 4:16

Let us then approach God's throne of grace with confidence, so that we may receive mercy and find grace to help us in our time of need.

Knowing all this, we can come to the throne of grace with confidence!

At His throne, we will find *"mercy"* and *"grace"*

to help us in our time of need: "Mercy" is NOT getting what we DO deserve! "Grace" IS getting what we DON'T deserve! God's desire for those who will come to Him is to help them!

The throne of God is available. We can come with *"CONFIDENCE"* (NIV) or as the KJV has it, *"BOLDLY!"* We are told we can come boldly or with confidence even when we are struggling! God is our high priest who is touched by our experiences and struggles to fight against temptation. <u>He died to redeem us, not reject us</u>!

Matthew 4:1-4

¹ Then Jesus was led by the Spirit into the wilderness to be tempted by the devil. ² After fasting forty days and forty nights, he was hungry. ³ The tempter came to him and said, "If you are the Son of God, tell these stones to become bread."

⁴ Jesus answered, "It is written: 'Man shall not live on bread alone, but on every word that comes from the mouth of God.'"

The first temptation Jesus faced in the wilderness was the temptation to turn to material things to SATISFY His needs. Ironically, this was basically Israel's early test in the wilderness as well, having to do with food and water. Israel griped about the *"heavenly bread"* and wanted *"physical flesh"* instead. *They failed this test.* There certainly wasn't anything wrong with Jesus making a stone into bread to satisfy His natural hunger, but to do it at Satan's request would have been to get sidetracked from the real issue at hand. He was about to begin His earthly ministry, and natural bread was not supposed to be His focus. That is the focus of this world. The temptation here was to lose focus, from a spiritual one to a material one! This will be a constant struggle as we live as God's people in this world! While it might not have seemed like a big thing right at that moment, to start out with a focus on the material would certainly have led Jesus further and further away from His mission which was spiritual in nature!

We don't always see the price of yielding to temptation all at once. It is usually a gradual process that takes us from point "A" to point "B" in a process that moves us away from God. Jesus avoids the temptation to start down the road of material appetites, for this would have corrupted His mission in the end!

Notice how Jesus *"holds firm to His faith"* ... *"Man does not live by bread alone, but by every word that comes from the mouth of God."* (Matt. 4:4) Heavenly bread is far more important than physical bread! Israel got sick of the *"bread from heaven"* (manna) — God provided it for them for every day to meet their full needs, but they tired of it! Jesus never tired of the Word of God and let us never tire of it either! The church and the Christian will always be in trouble when it turns away from the Scriptures, when the Word of God is diminished, and the needs of human flesh are the focus. When this happens, we are in trouble!

Christ's security was not in physical bread, it was in the Word of God! Since Jesus fought off this first temptation with Scripture and won, we can too since the same thing is still available for us today! You will always do well to win over temptation if you have the Word of God ready at hand! Jesus doesn't use tricks or fancy miracles to beat this temptation, He doesn't exercise His power as God, He uses the Word of God, and in doing so showed that we have the same power as He did! If Jesus had resisted in any other way, He could not have been an example to us, but because He used the same resource available to us, we have no excuse.

Matthew 4:5-7

⁵ Then the devil took him to the holy city and had him stand on the highest point of the temple. ⁶ "If you are the Son of God," he said, "throw yourself down. For it is written: 'He will command his angels concerning you, and they will lift you up in their hands, so that you will not strike your foot against a stone.'"

⁷ Jesus answered him, "It is also written: 'Do not put the Lord your God to the test.'"

Jesus now faced the second temptation. This is perhaps the greatest temptation for people in the church today, to choose the *spectacular* rather than the *Scripture!* It is interesting to see how Jesus used miracles. Most of the time He did a miracle He instructed those who received it to *"go and tell no one!"* Many times, Jesus refused to do miracles because the crowd came just for that reason! In this passage Jesus said it was a *"wicked generation that seeks for signs"* – and the only sign He would give was the sign of Jonah, the image of three days and nights in the bowels of the earth – fulfilled in Christ's death and resurrection! The focus of Jesus' ministry was basic: *"repent and be saved!"* Like a man named Billy Graham who has had no spectacular miracles accredited to his ministry except the millions who have found Christ as savior – he kept the message basic and focused! John the Baptist was said by Jesus in Luke 7:28 to be the greatest man born of woman – yet in John 10:41 it says, *"Though John never performed a miraculous sign, all that John said about this man was true."* (Referring to Jesus) John the Baptist never did perform a single recorded miracle – he only preached the Gospel, and Jesus said that *"no man was born greater among women than John!"* (Matt. 11:11; Luke 7:28) It can be easy to lose sight of what is important!

Jesus is being asked by Satan to do some

extraordinary miracle that will *"wow"* the crowds at the Temple – then He could avoid all the mundane efforts or daily traveling, working, and preaching, the day-by-day hard work of ministry that has little shine to it. Jesus' miracles certainly did attract crowds, but they never kept them for long! While the crowds often followed Jesus excitably after He did a miracle, as soon as He began to teach repentance and faith, to give a glass of cold water, to visit the sick or those in prison, to clothe the naked, to bind up the broken-hearted, to forgive others, and yes even to tithe – then we read that the crowds left! Remember in John 6 after the crowds were awed by Jesus, Jesus said that they must *"eat His flesh and drink His blood"* or they could have no part in Him – read John 6:66, *"From this time many of His disciples turned back and no longer followed Him!"*

It is also interesting to note that one of the characteristics of the last days will be *"signs and wonders"* – both from God and from the deceiver! Hence in 1 John 4:1 we are called upon to *"test the spirits."* The Bible even talks about the elect being led astray if that were possible, simply meaning that this undo emphasis on signs and wonders can even draw aside Christians if we don't stay on guard. Jesus even talked about those who will do miracles in His name (Matt. 7:21) but not necessarily be living for Him. He declares about these miracle workers that *"I never knew you!"* Miracles done even in Jesus' name don't necessarily indicate the godliness of those who "do them" – the message they bring does this!

MIRACLES are not a guarantee that something is right – but the MESSAGE OF GOD'S WORD about Jesus Christ is always right!

In Matthew 11:20 we read this: *"Then Jesus began to denounce the cities in which most of His miracles had been performed, BECAUSE THEY DID NOT REPENT."* Salvation was Jesus' goal, not performing signs and wonders for the crowds to be awed over.

Note how the crowds were not much different for the Apostles: In Acts 14:8-20 we read about Paul and Barnabus having just laid hands on a lame man, and he was healed – the crowd went crazy and started to worship Paul and Barnabus as two gods, Zeus, and Hermes! The Apostles had a hard time trying to get the crowd to accept them as humans when along came a few Jews that turned the crowds against Paul and Barnabas (Acts 14:19) so quickly that they stoned Paul and left him for dead! How fickle the crowd was – they liked being wowed, but not confronted for their sins!

It is so much easier to look for the spectacular and miss the obvious!

Jesus was facing a tough, hard road, many days of ordinary ministry punctuated by times of great events. How tempting to bypass the everyday, ordinary stuff by doing something spectacular before the crowd at the Temple! A spectacular miracle would "wow" them right off and save Him lots of time establishing the fact that He was the Messiah! Remember, these three temptations are taking place just as He is about to start His public ministry! The lure was to avoid the basic stuff, go for the spectacular! <u>Satan will use the "spectacular" in the last days to deceive people. We have got to know the "message!"</u>

Jesus once again defeats this temptation with the Word of God: *"Do not test the Lord your God."* In other words, don't even think you can bribe God into avoiding the message of the cross! It is noteworthy also that Satan never did quote the whole verse of Scripture when he attempted to use the Bible to tempt Jesus! He conveniently left a part of the passage out! It is the WHOLE of the Bible we need to adhere to keep from false doctrine!

Matthew 4:8-11

[8] Again, the devil took him to a very high mountain and showed him all the kingdoms of the world and their splendor. [9] "All this I will give you," he said, "if you will bow down and worship me."
[10] Jesus said to him, "Away from me, Satan! For it is written: 'Worship the Lord your God, and serve him only.'"
[11] Then the devil left him, and angels came and attended him.

The final temptation represented the desire for a "shortcut" to the RIGHT goal! Jesus would be Lord over all the kingdoms of this earth! Satan merely states here that since Jesus is going to get them anyway, why not let Satan give them to Him now and avoid the cross altogether! This is the *"ends justify the means"* problem of our society today! *"What difference does it make how we get there as long as the end result is good!"*

All Jesus had to do was bow *"once"* and worship Satan! How many bows to Satan does it take to lose? ONE! The temptation here was to avoid all the pain and suffering, all day-by-day efforts, all the routine servanthood stuff, just take the kingdoms now! This is the heart of the world, avoid sacrifice, suffering, serving ... *"just give me the reward now!"* The temptation here is to see the "ORDINARY" as somehow not the EXTRAORDINARY ... YET IT IS!

This temptation to take a "shortcut" is very real, and many take it today! There are no shortcuts to holy living – it takes effort, daily routine serving, faithfulness, all over protracted periods of time! It takes time and work to build a healthy ministry, to be a healthy Christian, to do a fruitful work for God. It doesn't come in an instant like many of the instant things we have in society today! There are *"no shortcuts to glory!"*

Jesus wins the day again through the Scriptures, and so can we! Jesus fought every temptation with the written Word of God – the same source of fighting Satan's temptations is available to us! If Jesus had used some other power to resist Satan besides the Word of God, then we could not have seen Him as a high priest. We would not be able to identify with Him had He used His powers as God, but because He used the Word of God, we have the same Word to use today that He used to win!

This is how we "HOLD FIRM TO THE FAITH!" In the last days the Bible says, *"Those things which can be shaken will be shaken" (*Heb. 12:27-28) – only those who have a firm grasp on God's Word are going to be able to walk a clear path! If we lay hold of God's Word it will lay hold of us! Avoid the shortcuts! *"<u>Let us Hold Firmly to the Faith</u>!"*

People lose their firm faith when two things happen: They think they are alone without help, and they lose focus on Christ and His Word! Christ offers a remedy for both problems: He can understand us and offers help. And He shows us by example how to keep the focus!

Are you firm or flimsy in your faith? *"LET US HOLD FIRMLY TO THE FAITH!"*

Entering God's Presence

Hebrews 5:1-14

Fear can be a devastating thing! When we are not confident in something or someone, we feel fearful, and this can keep us from moving forward in life. One really great example of this was after World War II in the story told of a Japanese soldier by the name of Shoichi Yokoi who lived in a cave on the island of Guam to which he fled in 1944 when the tides of war began to change. Fearing for his life, he stayed hidden for twenty-eight years in the jungle cave, coming out only at night. During this self-imposed exile he lived on frogs, rats, snails, shrimp, nuts, and mangoes. Even when he figured out the war was over he was afraid to come out for fear he would be executed. Two hunters found him one day and escorted him to freedom. He was living all this time under the indictment of sins that had all been dealt with – but he simply had not appropriated the atonement that was available

In the same way many people view God as a fearsome and frightening entity. They either believe God doesn't care or doesn't exist, or if He does, He is unapproachable. This is so far from the picture we have of Christ in the Bible, in fact, the opposite is true – Jesus Christ is not only approachable, but He also literally experienced our humanity, including temptations to sin in order to become a perfect high priest to help us, and to heal us from our sinful ways.

No human being other than Jesus Christ can offer to mediate between God and man. If they are just another human being they are flawed and don't even know what it means to stand in God's presence – they therefore can't qualify as our mediator. And God the Father is so perfect that we could never stand in His direct presence as we are, for we are sinners. Christ therefore became a living breathing fully human being and experienced our humanity without sinning so He could offer Himself up as both our mediator and sacrifice. In doing this He proved God's love toward us; He would *"die for us while we were yet sinners!"* He also understands our frailty and can be our perfect high priest to enable us to come into God's presence *"BOLDLY!"* (KJV) or with great *"CONFIDENCE"* (NIV).

The Bible teaches us that we can enter God's presence boldly through Christ who has not only paid the price for our sins, but acts as our perfect high priest. It is possible to experience God's love and forgiveness, mercy and grace, and new life through Christ.

Matthew 4:14-16

^{14} to fulfill what was said through the prophet Isaiah: ^{15} "Land of Zebulun and land of Naphtali, the Way of the Sea, beyond the Jordan, Galilee of the Gentiles— ^{16} the people living in darkness have seen a great light."

The conclusion of *"Therefore…"* here states categorically that we have a great high priest in Jesus Christ! Jesus never sinned, He was 100% human and 100% God. This makes Him unique in history – and makes it possible for us to have a relationship with God through Him. Why did Jesus willingly die in our place? Because *"He so loved the world ..."* He wanted us to have fellowship with God, and the only way for that to happen was for the price of sin to be paid fully for mankind. Jesus bore that price though He Himself was sinless and perfect. What does this mean? It means that it is possible now through Christ to be in right relationship with God! It also means that we can come into God's presence BOLDLY or with great CONFIDENCE! Christ bore our sins and our humanity, and by becoming one of us, He changed forever the way we see God and the way God sees us! How can we resist this kind of love?

God's plan wasn't just forgiveness and freedom from penalty, it was intended to restore us to God's favor through Christ! This is why we can come boldly or confidently into God's presence. We are now *"sons and daughters of the Highest God!"* Imagine the change of heart this creates, especially when we know we are still flawed and sinful at times!

Christ becoming our perfect high priest and

dying for our sins and restoring us to favor with God creates a boldness and confidence that far exceeds our own knowledge of the flawed characters we know we really are! When we come to God we don't do so based on how WE feel, but we come based on how GOD feels about us! This is an important distinction! Yes, we know we still mess up – and when we do we still need to repent; but we belong to God through Christ's sacrificial work and God our Father sees us through the blood of Christ, not the weakness of our humanity.

This knowledge that Christ died for us and paid our way back to God's favor should invigorate our value and our love in the eyes of God. And by the way, this should not lead to being sloppy about sin. When one realizes what Christ has done and is so moved by this act of love, it creates a desire in our heart to NOT SIN, but to live up to what Christ has made us, sons and daughters of God! If it leads to being casual about sin or not taking sin seriously in our lives then we have not truly appreciated what Christ has done for us, in fact, we are cheapening the sacrifice of Jesus for us!

When we come boldly into His presence, now we

know we can find mercy and help – precisely what the Hebrew writer says in Hebrews 4:16b. We need not fear coming to God! We can come boldly!

Hebrews 5:1-3

¹ Every high priest is selected from among the people and is appointed to represent the people in matters related to God, to offer gifts and sacrifices for sins. ² He is able to deal gently with those who are ignorant and are going astray, since he himself is subject to weakness. ³ This is why he has to offer sacrifices for his own sins, as well as for the sins of the people.

If you were going to stand in the presence of the Supreme Court of the United States of America you would want to have the finest legal representation possible, after all – you will be standing in the presence of the greatest judges on earth! Now take that even further, if you are going to stand before the Judge of the universe, God Himself – you will want the finest representation possible as well!

Unfortunately, there are no human beings qualified to stand in as your representative from earth! And I wouldn't recommend you representing yourself in the greatest court in eternity! *(Lawyers often refer to people who decide to represent themselves as "having fools for representation.")* Jesus however becomes our representative before His Father, and this is the greatest representative you could ever hope to have! Jesus and Jesus alone is capable of allowing you to pass the test before God, and even find favor and approval from God the Father!

Doesn't it make sense to have the best source possible when facing the greatest test for eternity? There is a way to stand confidently and boldly in God's presence! His name is Jesus Christ – and He is the chosen representative for all humans to come to God with confidence. There are no others!

Hebrews 5:4-5

[4] And no one takes this honor on himself, but he receives it when called by God, just as Aaron was.
[5] In the same way, Christ did not take on

himself the glory of becoming a high priest.
But God said to him,
"You are my Son; today I have become your Father."

There have always been people in history that have claimed they will save the world, they will build great empires, they will solve mankind's problems. Some of them disguised their ambitions in the early stages by appearing to unite and strengthen their countrymen, people like Hitler, Stalin, Mussolini, Alexander the Great, Napoleon, etc. However, all these turned out to be despots, bent on usurping power over others, flawed and full of sin that drove them in the end to be exposed for who they really were. God never picked any of them – although some claimed that right in their early stages of power.

There is only ONE who was chosen by God in all of history to bring restoration to mankind; and instead of amassing power for Himself, He willingly died for everyone else, including accepting the penalty of sin though He Himself never sinned! Just as in the Old Covenant, one did not appoint himself as high priest; it was revealed by God who would serve in this role! Any attempts to usurp that role ended in death! The author of Hebrews states the same here for Christ, *"No one takes the honor upon himself; he must be called by God, just as Aaron was."* So Christ also did not take upon Himself the glory of becoming a high priest. God called Him, chose Him, and revealed Him! There was no other name throughout time!

This is why we must learn that it is ONLY in the name of Christ that we can come to God and find favor! God has set this up. It does not matter if it is logical or politically correct – God said only through His Son and this name shall mankind be saved! The early church and leaders clearly understood this. We read in Acts 4:12, *"Salvation is found in no one else, for there is no other name under heaven given to men by which we must be saved!"* <u>All roads DO NOT lead to God</u>! But coming to God through Christ gives you great favor, favor you would not get otherwise in any other way, by any other means!

Hebrews 5:6-10

> *⁶ And he says in another place, "You are a priest forever, in the order of Melchizedek."*
> *⁷ During the days of Jesus' life on earth, he offered up prayers and petitions with fervent cries and tears to the one who could save him from death, and he was heard because of his reverent submission. ⁸ Son though he was, he learned obedience from what he suffered ⁹ and, once made perfect, he became the source of eternal salvation for all who obey him ¹⁰ and was designated by God to be high priest in the order of Melchizedek.*

Jesus did not simply come and throw around His power as the Son of God, instead He laid down those powers willingly and prayed, submitted, and lived out a life of Holy living by the power of the Holy Spirit – the same power available to us as well. Jesus learned obedience through suffering; all of this He did not have do, He was already God – but He knew that without becoming fully man and dying for us there would be no reconciliation with God. He also knew no one else could do this. So, He willingly accepted this role out of love to redeem mankind from its own foolish ways. What the first Adam destroyed, Jesus who in the New Testament is called the second Adam restored! Jesus succeeded where Adam and Eve failed.

THERE IS NO OTHER RELIGION ON EARTH WHERE GOD HIMSELF PAID THE PRICE, SUFFERED AND DIED FOR US. In other religions you have to try and find God; you have to follow certain rituals and paths. In some religions those gods never died for man. Their gods are elusive – you can only hope to find nirvana eventually, or if you worked hard enough maybe you would get paradise, etc. Only in Christianity does God take the penalty of sin, only in Christianity does God die for us, and only in Christianity does God in Christ actually defeat death and rise again from the dead. Only in Christianity does God take the bullet for us!

With all this in mind, how can you not feel confident to come into God's very presence, and feel bold about doing so? There is great resource in finding compassion, mercy, forgiveness, help and love, joy, and peace in coming to God through Christ who is a high priest touched with our feelings of weakness! We don't come to God in Christ with fear of being pushed away, or of God having little interest in us – we can come confidently because we know that with Christ as our sacrifice and high priest we can enter confidently, even boldly into God's presence and we will not only be heard, but ministered to as well. God loves us and desires our best, our cleansing from sin, our healing and hopes restored. In times of blessings we can come gratefully before Him. In times of distress we can come confidently before Him knowing we will find mercy and help in our time of need. So – *"Let us then approach the throne of grace with confidence, so that we may receive mercy and find grace to help us in our time of need!"* (Heb. 4:16)

We are not only invited into God's presence freely through Christ, we are encouraged to come *"boldly"* (KJV) – with *"confidence"* (NIV) into God's presence. In spite of who we are, when we come into God's presence through Christ our high priest and sacrifice, we actually enter into God's presence with God desiring to grant us mercy and grace to help us! It is not earned by our "goodness" – it is given by Christ's work on our behalf. Are you coming boldly to God, are you confident of your heavenly Father's love for you? *"LET US GO WITH CONFIDENCE ..."*

There has been a dramatic shift in our society over the past generation. We have gone from a sense of duty and responsibility to a demand for services and entertainment. The society around us has put great emphasis on *"how do you feel?"* as being more important that *"what should we do?"* Our society has turned inward rather than outward, a reflection of self-absorption and immaturity.

It is tragic, but the church can reflect society all too much. Probably the weakness of churches today is that they fail to challenge those Christians in the congregation to move on to maturity. If we are not careful we will strive to make people HAPPY rather than make them HOLY, that we will make them FEEL GOOD rather than make them FAITHFUL & GODLY. We must be careful not to encourage just EXCITEMENT and avoid EDUCATION spiritually.

The story is told about an old American Indian who attended a church service one Sunday morning. The preacher's message lacked real spiritual food, so he did a lot of shouting and pulpit pounding to cover up his lack of preparation. In fact, as it is sometimes said, he "preached up quite a storm." After the service, someone asked the Indian, who was a Christian, what he thought of the minister's message. Thinking for a moment, he summed up his opinion in six words: "High wind. Big thunder. No rain." Yes, when the Scriptures are neglected, there is "no rain." Only when preaching is based on God's Word and His people are challenged to respond and be responsible to that Word are they blessed and refreshed.

Excitement, feeling good, even entertainment can certainly be a part of our experience as a Christian, but it must not be a substitute for spiritual maturity.

While there is an appropriate time to be immature as a Christian, we must not stay in such a state. If our children never physically matured in the years after their birth we would take them to a doctor to see what was wrong. If our children never matured emotionally we would take them to a counselor. Why is it we will ignore the lack of spiritual maturity in our lives?

The Bible clearly teaches us that Christ wants us to move toward a mature walk with God. It is not enough to just get saved and wait for the rapture of the church. Growth should be a normal part of our walk with God.

Hebrews 5:7-8

[7] During the days of Jesus' life on earth, he offered up prayers and petitions with fervent cries and tears to the one who could save him from death, and he was heard because of his reverent submission. [8] Son though he was, he learned obedience from what he suffered.

Christ is the perfect example of maturity, but it is interesting to read here that even He *"learned obedience"* (Heb. 5:8) – growth came through being stretched! The obvious statements here have to do with "serving." Maturity is a process of taking the focus off ourselves and putting it on others.

How do we mature? Jesus was a student of the Scriptures. Jesus was not ruled by emotions. He did not avoid them either – Hebrews 5:7, *"During the days of Jesus' life on earth, he offered up prayers and petitions with loud cries and tears to the one who could save him from death, and he was heard because of his reverent submission."* As was expressed in this verse, Jesus offered up loud cries and tears. He was emotional! Jesus however wasn't ruled by those emotions. Jesus' focus was not His own needs, but those of others. Jesus' motivation was not from how He would benefit; it was motivated by His love for others and His duty to His heavenly Father.

The writer here first gives us a picture of Jesus so that when he makes the statement that they needed to move on to maturity they would know what that means! Jesus sets for us the emphasis for growing spiritually. His focus is outward, what He can do to minister. Servants in the Kingdom of God are those who are growing. Those who fail to serve rarely grow spiritually! Jesus' focus on His disciples was similar. While He did teach them, He also washed their feet and served and called them to do the same. Teaching without connected responsibilities leads to intellectual arrogance. Even our school systems are becoming aware of this principle; many of them have included community service as a requirement for graduation. There must be a connection between what we know and what we do! Too many times some of the most difficult Christians to deal with are those who like to argue Scripture but don't have their own life together! The Pharisees were great theologians and had command of large portions of Scripture, but Jesus said they made their disciples *"twice the son of Hell"* as they were (Matt. 23:15). Their prayers and their service was done to be seen of men, not out of service to God! Sometimes the loudest complainers are the least involved in ministry! It is time to grow up!

Christ's perfect example of maturity should be our example for growth. He set His heart to serve and sacrifice, and we should do no less. The more mature a person is the more willing that person is to do what is needed, not just what they feel like doing. There are no shortcuts to maturity, or instant ways of getting there!

Hebrews 5:9-10

⁹ and, once made perfect, he became the source of eternal salvation for all who obey him [10] and was designated by God to be high priest in the order of Melchizedek.

These statements indicate that Jesus was unwavering by experiences in life. Both good and bad, they did not change his commitment to the Father or to us. One of the prevailing characteristics of mature people is that they are stable. Mature people are not starting and quitting all the time based on how they feel at the time. They are people who have learned to handle the bumps in life and stay on course.

Jesus never altered course, even in Gethsemane when he was in *"great distress"* and sweated as it were great drops of blood from the struggle. He still stayed the course, praying, *"not my will but thine be done."* Maturity takes guts! Maturity takes strength! It takes very little work to be immature, but it takes great energy to be mature and stay stable!

Some Christians are always floating around looking for something to meet their expectations and wants. Others keep plugging away looking for needs and trying to make things better. Look at Jesus. He did not try and reject Judaism, He continued to pray and preach at the synagogues though they were wrong. He sought to bring the Jews the truth and change them. It was the Pharisees that rejected Christ. Maturity means dealing with things, not running away from them.

A wise man of the Orient once remarked: "There are three kinds of people in all types of organizations – rowboat people, sailboat people, and steamboat people. Rowboat people need to be pushed or shoved along. Sailboat people move when a favorable wind is blowing. Steamboat people move continuously, through calm or storm. They usually are masters of themselves, their surroundings, and their fate."

Christ's example for us to follow is that of stability.

Hebrews 5:11-14

[11] We have much to say about this, but it is hard to make it clear to you because you no longer try to understand. [12] In fact, though by this time you ought to be teachers, you need someone to teach you the elementary truths of God's word all over again. You need milk,

> not solid food! ¹³ Anyone who lives on milk, being still an infant, is not acquainted with the teaching about righteousness. ¹⁴ But solid food is for the mature, who by constant use have trained themselves to distinguish good from evil.

The writer of Hebrews would go on more about Christ's example and His Melchizedek-like Priesthood, but he explains that they are not in a place at this time to do that. They have been too comfortable not growing. In fact he states that they need to return to the elementary teachings again! Whoever these early Christians were, they were not growing! In fact, the writer seems to imply that they had done nothing since they got saved except to simply exist! They were happy just being saved and had done nothing to learn more and grow! These were strong words for this group. These people however were not just recent converts. These were people who had been saved for some time but had not gone on in their walk with God. They were comfortable and secure, so they were not growing! This group no doubt was offended by this challenge and correction; immature people usually do get offended when their immaturity is highlighted. The author is challenging the fact that they were still infants spiritually; as long as they have been saved they should be on solid food and not spiritual milk anymore! Immature people usually get quite uncomfortable around mature people!

A person can be a Christian for many years yet remain spiritually immature. Therefore, it's possible for a new believer to be far more grown up in the Lord than someone who has been saved for 40 years. A good example of this is found in an incident described by Ethel Barrett in her book, *It Only Hurts When I Laugh*. She said that when D.L. Moody became a Christian, he developed such a hunger for God's Word, spent so much time reading it, and was so quick to obey it that he became a "menace" to some believers. His rapid spiritual growth was an embarrassment to certain people who, though they had been saved for years, never grew up in Christ. Week after week in the church Moody attended, he would share a new experience he had with the Lord. Finally, some of the older saints who just couldn't stand feeling humiliated by his exemplary life went to Moody's uncle and urged him to quiet down his nephew. Ethel Barrett drew this conclusion about Moody: "His robust spiritual health and bounding energy disturbed their napping; he was just too much. So, while they were sucking their thumbs, he was growing until he left them far behind; he grew more in a few years than they did in thirty."

Maturity is a choice, not an automatic thing in the spiritual realm! Our lives should reflect growth. We cannot grow if we don't even master the basics first! We shouldn't be afraid to challenge each other to grow! One pastor I know told me that if he told his people to tithe they would get mad and be offended! Paul wrote to Timothy and said that "leadership" in the church should not be given to "novices" (new Christians) because they would be too immature and thus not able to handle the stress or give a proper example for others to follow. Leaders were to be those tested and "proved" to be mature.

Creating a Firm Foundation

Hebrews 6:1-3, 9-12

Make sure you have mastered the elementary things of God before trying to delve into the deep mysteries of God!

Hebrews 6:1-3

¹ Therefore let us move beyond the elementary teachings about Christ and be taken forward to maturity, not laying again the foundation of repentance from acts that lead to death, and of faith in God,
² instruction about cleansing rites, the laying

on of hands, the resurrection of the dead, and eternal judgment. ³ And God permitting, we will do so.

The author's words here are a challenge – a challenge to move on and not just be satisfied with the elementary things of God, the basics!

Hebrews 6:9-12

⁹ Even though we speak like this, dear friends, we are convinced of better things in your case—the things that have to do with salvation. ¹⁰ God is not unjust; he will not forget your work and the love you have shown him as you have helped his people and continue to help them. ¹¹ We want each of you to show this same diligence to the very end, so that what you hope for may be fully realized. ¹² We do not want you to become lazy, but to imitate those who through faith and patience inherit what has been promised.

Notice in verse 12 he states that he doesn't want

them to become lazy and be satisfied; they are to press on. Like all Christians of all ages, they want to be mature, but they needed to be willing to pay the price to get there! They want a strong stable life, and they want it NOW – forgetting that maturity comes through a process that takes both time and effort!

Bill Hybels says, "You don't get a well-fed church from serving fast food."

It is not that we are always unsatisfied; it is that we are not satisfied to stay at immature stages on a permanent basis. There is a proper satisfaction that should come for whatever stage of growth we are in, but we must not be satisfied to stay there! Growth means maturing, a process for all of us. *"Let us mature"* – as we become more of a servant and take the focus off our own lives to see what God wants us to do for Him, we will grow. Maturity requires discipline and work, and any church that will move forward must have in it people and a pastor who are moving forward!

While physical growth is simply an automatic response to BODY CHEMISTRY, spiritual growth is a function of a BELIEVER'S CHOICES! Spiritual growth toward maturity should be the goal of every Christian, and it does not just "happen" to us. We must take an active role in facilitating it. If we take seriously the failure of a child growing physically or intellectually, shouldn't we take seriously the lack of spiritual growth in our own lives? Are you maturing?

Drawing Near to God

Hebrews 10:22-23

In the Old Testament it was very dramatic when God was approached. First, only the high priest could ever actually enter the Holy of Holies, and then only once a year. If he approached God's presence in an impure state or not properly cleansed, he would die immediately! It was almost scary to enter the Holy of Holies. Inside was the Ark of the Covenant and the Mercy Seat where the blood was to be sprinkled. The high priest would wear a bell around his ankle with a rope attached just in case he died going into God's presence. They could pull his body back out – no one else could enter or they would die. That one day a year when it was time for the high priest could go in and sprinkle blood for the remission of Israel's sins as well as the sins of the high priest must have been a very dramatic moment. Tension most likely filled the air and relief when the high priest returned alive!

How different under the New Covenant! Jesus serves as both high priest and as the blood sacrifice – as well as the Mercy Seat and Ark of the Covenant. In doing so He forever changed the way we approach God! This is GOOD NEWS! – the very meaning of the word "Gospel."

The Scriptures teach us that we have complete access to God through Jesus Christ and His sacrifice on the cross. Because our lives are cleansed by Christ's blood we can draw near to God with full assurance that He will receive us. This is so very different from the Old Testament era when approaching God was scary!

Hebrews 10:22

Let us draw near to God with a sincere heart and with the full assurance that faith brings, having our hearts sprinkled to cleanse us from a guilty conscience and having our bodies washed with pure water.

The lead in statement here is amazing – *"Let us draw near to God!"* To a Jewish audience this was an amazing statement! It was amazing because the very idea that anyone could approach God was nearly impossible under the Old Covenant. The writer here however is stating unequivocally that access to God is not only possible, we are encouraged to do so! God has granted access – through His son Jesus! How many people are missing out on God's presence because they simply do not know how available it is?

Sadly, so many people are not aware in their spiritual thirst that He who is *"living water"* is readily available and can quench their thirsty soul and grant access to the very presence of God Himself.

Sincerity is more than just a light emotion, it means to come to God with a genuine desire to be truthful with Him as well as truthful with ourselves. God does not do well with hypocrites! Jesus had some of the strongest words with hypocrites in His own day. Sincerity is more than just attempting to be honest, it is being honest! It is possible to be sincere and sincerely wrong too! It is thus more than a surface understanding of "sincerity" that is being spoken of here. The literal idea is *"with a truthful heart."* It is the idea of what Jesus meant when He said that those who wanted to worship God must worship Him in *"Spirit and in truth."* To be pure means to come sincerely.

A girl in Sunday school had read the Beatitudes in Matthew. She was asked which of the things mentioned she would most like to have. She said, "A pure heart." When asked why she preferred that, she said, "If my heart were pure, I believe I would have all the other virtues mentioned in this chapter."

The Lord never turned away from a sincere heart reaching out to him, whether it was a fallen woman of low regard, or people with addiction problems like drunkards, or those who were known sinners in his culture like tax collectors, etc. Whenever Jesus met someone who was truthful He reached out to them. He would go out of his way to spend time with a truthful sinner – like Zacchaeus. The woman at the well was another truthful person – although

Jesus had to kind of pull it out of her, but her sincere heart brought her into the light of God's saving grace. When we come with a sincere heart God grants full and quick access – always! It is a door opener.

It is important to note that assurance comes only with faith! This of course means that one cannot be assured of their place before God without faith, and indeed the writer of Hebrews said this in the next chapter, *"Without faith it is impossible to please God…"* (Heb. 11:6)

Our assurance is the result of Christ's sacrifice, and our faith in Him and that work He has done. Only when that faith is properly placed do we experience this absolute assurance. Sometimes it is hard to have faith, because things don't always work out the way we want them to or expect them to. But when that happens, that is exactly when our faith works best! And it is then when our faith gives us the greatest assurance! If we belong to Christ we need not fear anything that might come down the pike!

Faith brings this important assurance to our hearts and minds! We are His, and because of this we have full access to Him now as well as in the future.

Our hearts are clean when we come to Christ. He has acquitted us of all our sins by the work on Calvary through His death and resurrection. Guilty we could not come before His presence. Like the high priest in the Old Testament, entrance into the Holy of Holies with sin in their heart meant immediate death – but Christ's sacrifice was perfect, and His shed blood made possible our cleansing from all sins, and thus freedom to stand in His presence. It is important to realize that this cleansing is true whether we always feel it or not. Faith works in good times and bad times.

Faith on a full stomach may be simply contentment – but if you have it when you're hungry, it's genuine. No matter what we face in life, good things or bad things – we can face God at all times because we belong to Him, and He has cleansed us and acquitted us of all guilt and sin. We must never fear to come into His presence! We must always come with a cleansed heart. He will never push us aside.

No more guilty conscience when we have come to Christ. So many people hold on to their past sins, and by doing so they are robbing themselves of the joy of being saved! They also make it harder to come into the presence of God with a clear conscience when they don't allow their own forgiveness for past sins. Jesus made it pretty clear, when we come to Him and receive Him, ALL our sins are forgiven and we are "new" creatures – "born again." Old things pass away, all things become new! Approaching our Lord is supposed to be a thing of joy, not of fear! This is why the Bible states, *"Perfect love casts out all fear."* (1 John 4:18) The bottom line in an imperfect world is that we are the winners! This is true whether current realities seem to show that – we are tuned into another kingdom which will never lose or pass away.

We need to act and live like winners no matter what we are facing in life. God has already determined the outcome of our faith and that is eternity with Him! We can live in a fallen world like victors with a clean conscience – our sins have been taken away. This was symbolized even in the Old Covenant by the "scapegoat" that had the sins of Israel pronounced on its head, and then was led out into the desert to disappear. Once the high priest had confessed the sins of the people and made a blood sacrifice for them they were reminded that such sins disappeared forever. Why do so many Christians allow themselves to be trapped by their past? It is unnecessary and unproductive, and can spoil the joy of coming into God's presence.

Like the hit song in the recent animated movie *Frozen* says, "Let it go, let it go, let it go." It will be hard to "draw near to God" if we cling to our past sins or guilt of them. The final statement in this verse clearly indicates a complete "washing." And washed with *"pure water."* It is not from human effort that this *"pure water"* springs; it is from the fountain of Christ's shed blood! Too many people think they have to earn their salvation, and that getting clean is a work of their own power. It is NOT our power; it is God's power and cleansing! When we falsely assume it is up to our ability to cleanse ourselves from our sins we will discover that it is nearly impossible!

God desires us to come to Him, He calls us to fellowship with Him, He has made the way possible, He has paid the price, He has opened the way – all through the work and sacrifice of His son Jesus. Why would you hesitate to come to a God who has done all the work, paid the price for all sin, and beckoned you to come to Him? Jesus said this during His ministry on earth, *"Come to me, all you who are weary and burdened, and I will give you rest."* (Matt. 11:28) Unlike other religions on this earth, all but one make it up to you to earn your way. With some you have to beat yourself, or try and discipline yourself to earn God's favor. Some teach that you will not likely ever reach "nirvana" in this life, but keep trying. Some teach you have to prove yourself by forcing others to submit. There is only one "religion" however where God says, "Come ... I've done it all for you," and that is Christianity. It isn't about how good you can be for God to love you; it is about how good God is that He loves you! How can anyone resist the love Jesus Christ showed by taking the price of sin upon Himself?

The writer of Hebrews was writing to a people who had always known fear in coming to God. They had understood by the Old Covenant that approaching God was a frightening thing. All of that was because Christ had not yet died as the perfect sacrifice and as our high priest. Now that He has come, entrance into the very presence of God is wide open. COME!

Hebrews 10:23

Let us hold unswervingly to the hope we profess, for he who promised is faithful.

Hope has real power! People who lose hope lose the ability to face the future. Sometimes their entire existence fades into oblivion and despair, but hope can not only revive life, it can heal the damages of tragedy as well.

Hope powerfully transforms reality! The lack of hope does the same thing, only in reverse. We will never survive this world without hope beyond this world. So much of the history of great men and women was based on a greater hope than what they were experiencing.

Jesus came into a dark world where hopelessness was gripping the world, and though He was crucified He gave hope to those who follow Him that exceeds the realities of this world.

The Scriptures teach us that we can endure all

things through Christ who alone gives us hope. The greater the object of hope, the greater the hope in enduring whatever comes, and there is nothing greater than Christ Himself!

The Hebrew writer says it straight forward, *"Let us hold unswervingly to the hope we profess..."* If we profess our faith in Christ we must not back away from the hope that comes in holding onto that profession of faith. Notice that the author is saying we need to hold onto our hope *"unswervingly"* – we must not be unsteady in our confidence, or we will lose our hope. Remember that this is an invitation, *"Let us..."* – we must participate in the process of staying steady in our profession and our confidence. There are a lot of realities that can throw off our hope and confidence if we get our eyes off of the greater realities of Christ and Heaven!

The fact is that the only thing we can be certain of is the character and Word of God Himself! Since everything else in the universe is fading away and uncertain, we can only hope in Christ who is eternal and everlasting. He is the one thing we can hope in without failure. It may seem at times that it is tough to trust in Him when we can't see what's coming, but in those times we still be unswerving in our hope and faith as the Lord guides us along one step at a time.

Sometimes we follow with limited vision and clarity, but nonetheless God is at work and leading us faithfully. Our hope is in Him, not our circumstances or ability to always see clearly. And it is in following Him when we can't see clearly that we live a steady life of hope and faith.

Hope is what gives us strength daily! Hope gives you the ability to stay strong in the midst of difficulties and trials, even when you don't see the end result. It is a confidence or hope in the very character of God Himself!! He is always good! He is always faithful! He is always powerful!

This allows us to feel strength even in the midst of circumstances that would otherwise drain our strength.

There is healing power in hope, because our hope is in Christ who is the great healer! History is replete with examples of people who have withstood horrible circumstances simply because they held onto hope. The disciples of Jesus often didn't understand all that Jesus taught them, but they learned to have hope in everything He said.

Hope keeps people from quitting, from giving up – because they still have hope! No wonder the writer here refers to *"holding unswervingly onto the hope."*

"For He who promised..." – God has not given us false hope, but real hope!

Hope is not based on what we decide we would like to see, it is based on real statements and realities that God Himself has promised us. So how do we know that these promises of God can be trusted? Christ was born a baby and experienced our entire humanity! Christ lived a sinless and righteous life! Christ rose again and met with His disciples and promised them that with the same power He rose from the dead He will come again and give them everything He told them about! His very resurrection proves He has both the power and the will to fulfill those promises. Though we can't always see through life's cloudy circumstances, God has a clear view of everything and the power to uphold us if we hold to that hope!

During World War II a father who was holding his son by the arm was seen running from a building that had just been bombed. In the front yard was a huge hole where a bomb had already exploded. Seeking shelter the father jumped into the hole and called for his son to jump down into his arms. The boy however, standing at the rim, could not see into the hole because of the dust and darkness, but the father could easily see the silhouette of his son against the sky above him. The boy hesitated and said, "But I can't see you, Dad," and the father responded, "That's o.k., son, I can see you and I won't let you fall, just jump!" In those times when we can't see the Father we must learn to trust Him to be there anyway. Prior experience with the Father will make it easier to jump when we need to.

Even facing death we still have hope, for we know the one who has overcome death and promised us that we will never die, but live forever with Him.

The final statement of this verse is as good a guarantee as can be! *"...for He who has promised is faithful."* And please note that the emphasis for hope is not on YOU, it is on HIM! If it was determined by our sheer will, we would be in trouble, but the guarantee that makes our hope rock solid is the fact that all that is promised is based on Christ and His work, not ours! Too often people want proof before they have faith or will act in faith; but real hope is when we act with or without the proofs apparent, based on simply the Word of God Himself.

It is important to act on our hope, otherwise it isn't real hope. Hope that shows itself in despair isn't real hope, it is a false hope! We must hold on to hope if we want it to change the way we live life.

Abraham Lincoln said, "Faith is not believing that God can, but that God will!"

We can face life – and death with hope because our hope is built on nothing less than the person and work of Jesus Christ and His faithfulness. *"He who promised is faithful!"*

"Let us hold unswervingly to the hope..."

Hope is a very powerful and very real thing! When people lose "hope" they lose the ability to continue on, to believe that life has meaning, that it makes any difference how we live. Often those who lose hope lose the will to live or fight. Hopelessness too can make someone ill or prevent someone from recovering from tragedy. However, if this is true the opposite is also true. Hope restores, renews, strengthens, and motivates someone to face the future with certainty and strength. If we are to go through this life victoriously, we must hold onto our hope without hesitation! Keep Hope Alive!

Lifting Up Others

Hebrews 10:24

Have you ever been provoked to anger? Probably we have all had that experience. It usually involves someone deliberately working hard to get under our skin, to not only show their contempt for us, but to move us to respond in kind. All of this of course with the intent of causing pain and hurt. In such cases the person who can get that kind of reaction from us feels powerful and in control. They may also feel a sick sense of relief at getting even.

What if we did this in reverse? Instead of provoking someone to anger, we used the same kind of emotional strength and strategy to provoke others to love and good works. This is behind this single verse of Scripture as the third exhortation in

Hebrews 10. The invitation to *"Let us..."* is meant to invite all the believers into a process of deliberate action toward others that will move them to love more, and to do good works out of joy. The more we combine our acts of love and good works, the more we move the world toward Christ! We may think our own small contribution won't matter, but when added to other believers we can show the power of God's love.

Hebrews 10:24

And let us consider how we may spur one another on toward love and good deeds,

The story is told of a heavy bronze bell that had sunk into a river in China. The efforts of various engineers to raise it had been of no avail. At last a clever native priest asked permission to make the attempt on the condition that the bell should be given to his temple. He then had his assistants gather an immense number of bamboo rods. These are hollow, light, and practically unsinkable. They were taken down by divers, one by one, and fastened to the bell. After many thousands of them had been thus fastened, it was noticed that the bell began to move, and, when the last one had been added, the buoyancy of the accumulated rods was so great that they actually lifted the enormous mass of bronze to the surface. You may think your bamboo rod is too small and light to make any difference, but it is necessary in God's sight to help in lifting souls to God and to lend strength to the others.

The Bible teaches us that we are to not only be full of love and good works, but we are to help spur on or provoke others to love and good works.

The author is using an unexpected word here, *"paroxusmon"* in Greek, translated here *"provoke."* This word was normally used in a negative sense, such as in provocation or exasperation toward anger! This may indicate that the believers were already "provoking" one another in negative ways, such as in arguing, or disagreements, perhaps building toward hatred – and so the author uses the same word to tell them STRONGLY to provoke each other toward love instead. In other words the author is saying, *"With the same energy you are using to provoke each other negatively, use it to do good instead!"*

The author of Hebrews does this in a very pastoral way. He says, *"LET US ..."* so he includes himself; it is not just aimed at them. All believers need to be cognizant of their own actions toward others, not to provoke to evil, but to provoke toward good. Discipline of life and love. They are to take notice of how their interactions affect each other. We can help people down a path of love or hurt them down a path of pain. Any attitude or action taken by us should be viewed through the lens of how it will affect others. Does it move others into the arena of being built up, or pulling them down? The idea is to go even beyond the "average" response, to actually go out of the way to do good to others, whether they deserve it or not!

When you fall in love with someone else, that is your only desire. You are provoked or excited to see how you can show your love to the one who is loved. This is natural when we fall in love with someone! Falling in love with someone will provoke us to do everything we can to show it! There should be the same attitude toward others when the love of Christ is ruling in our hearts! The Christian life doesn't just happen, it comes as the fruit of self-discipline along with God's graces. The focus here is a call to action, not just thought.

We cannot assume that Christian graces will *"just happen"* in our lives; they need to be developed. We need to *"work out our salvation with fear and trembling"* (Phil. 2:12b). Intentionality is involved here, as well as discipline. The writer is speaking about the effort of choice. They will need to stop "provoking" out of emotional responses, but rather start taking seriously their new status as believers and guide their beliefs and behaviors to be those that would "provoke" one another toward good works, not evil deeds. If in their past lives they provoked one another to hatred and anger, in their new life in Christ they are to use the same energy and zeal to "provoke" each other to love and good deeds. By doing this they will enable others to do the same. Their combined efforts will help them all!

The kind of love they are being asked to provoke is the word *"agape"* – the deepest kind of love. *"To consider"* provoking means to become deliberate at both thought and action how they could move each other forward in their hearts and minds and actions. To take self out of the front position and put others there instead. The concept of them provoking one another is almost akin to making a contest to see how they can outdo each other in moving people by love and good work. This shows how important good works are! It is not good works to *get* you saved, but good works because you *are* saved! The fruit of showing their good deeds and provoking one another to doing good deeds will be others coming to Christ. It is a way we demonstrate to the world the reality of God's presence in our own lives!

We become students at loving others and spurring others on to love others. The Christian life is not a haphazard existence, it is meant to be one of purposeful living. The purpose in life is not to fulfill ones' own needs, but those of others. There was no doubt some in the church who were doing this, and the writing is trying to encourage the rest to join in, hence the *"LET US..."* A community of believers loving each other is a powerful draw. People are drawn to a church not at first because of doctrine or architecture, they are often drawn because they hear and see stories of people who genuinely love each other and are out working hard at doing good works.

Even Jesus equated works as evidence of what lies inside each of us, so much so that faith and works were connected. *"What good is it, my brothers, if a man claims to have faith but has no deeds? Can such faith save him?"* (James 2:14) The implied answer of course is "no."

The kingdom of God is judged as much by our actions as it is by our words. That is an awesome responsibility! Church is not just about worshipping God by a few songs and a sermon; it is also just as much about spurring each other on to love and do good works to give witness to the powerful change that has taken place in our lives, lives once ruled by self, selfishness, and sin.

A Christian or community of Christians who are set on fire to love others and to do good will be a community or church that doesn't have a hard time attracting others to join in. The power of the Gospel is reflected through our love and those actions of love. So much so that Paul said to the Corinthians that even if we had supernatural abilities and supernatural gifts but did not have love we would be at best making a bunch of useless and powerless noise! Discipleship is not just *"learning"* Scripture, it is *"living"* Scripture! Even sinners have a hard time rejecting "good" people! This is not to be confused with goodness to earn God's favor. It is not that! It is goodness for God's sake!

A converted cowboy put it very well when he said, "Lots of folks that would really like to do right think that serving the Lord only means shouting themselves hoarse praising His name. Now I'll tell you how I look at that. I am working for Jim here. Now if I would do nothing but sit around the house telling what a good fellow Jim is and singing songs to him, I would not suit Jim. But when I buckle on my straps and hustle among the hills and see that Jim's herd is all right, not suffering for water and feed, or being driven off the range and branded by cow thieves, then I am serving Jim as he wants to be served." Let that be our philosophy, too, when the temptation is to talk instead of serving the Lord.

To be ambassadors of love to a suffering world, to do good to even those who would despitefully use us, that is power. The early church thrived though it was persecuted harshly because the early believers kept love in their hearts for sinners and kept good works as the normal outflow of everything they did. When the Roman Empire fell, Christianity moved forward because they won the day! What military power could not do, the power of God's love and believers who lived out faith by "being" good did. They established a kingdom greater than Rome! The path to revival in America isn't just some catchy campaign or large coliseum event, it is more about us "provoking" one another on to love and good works. So *"LET US...!"*

To impact the world for Christ will require us to consider how we can spur or provoke one another on toward love and good works. This does not cause faith to be brought down to the level of "good works" – rather it elevates good works to the level of faith! The existence of God's love is so powerful that it can't help but act in a positive way to others. Hebrews 10:24, *"And let us consider how we may spur one another on toward love and good deeds."*

Godly Discipline

Hebrews 12:1-27

If you have ever watched the Olympics on TV, you have probably been amazed at the feats the human body is capable of doing! It has always amazed me how some of these people have spent their entire childhood preparing for a single event that in some cases is over within a few minutes! The amount of training and sacrifice is enormous, all for a single goal – a gold medal and worldwide recognition that you are the best in that particular thing of all the humans on earth!

Since we are striving toward a more eternal reward, and more important recognition by God, are we as willing to make the appropriate sacrifices and practice the necessary disciplines? This is Paul's point in this passage *(or whoever wrote the book of Hebrews – another possible candidate is Barnabus)*. The writer has in mind the same kind of discipline that we witness every four years at the Olympics, for they existed as well in the Apostolic age.

We have a more important prize than mere gold, and more important recognition than just that of this world to consider. Are we taking seriously our walk with God?

Hebrews 12:1

Therefore, since we are surrounded by such a great cloud of witnesses, let us throw off everything that hinders and the sin that so easily entangles. And let us run with perseverance the race marked out for us,

The Bible teaches us that we must be prepared to examine and discipline our lives appropriately if we are to be a disciple of Christ. Salvation is not just a momentary experience at an altar, it is a lifestyle as well.

This is the meaning of the word for *"witnesses"*

used here. They are not the spectators of us, rather, they are the examples put before us – we are to look to them as they cheer us on! This is meant to be an encouragement – their examples witness to us that we can and should be fervent and faithful. We are literally surrounded by these examples: both Old Testament and New Testament as well as contemporary examples of faith. It is almost as if the writer here has in mind the champions mentioned in chapter 11 *(the faith chapter),* and like in the Olympics they are standing before us with their medals *(or wreaths)* and they are spurring us on to dream of winning too, thus encouraging us to strive by their examples. The example they set for us is to encourage us to *"throw off everything that hinders..."* The idea here is to encourage us who wish to win the race to get rid of those things that will slow us down or prevent us from competing seriously! The word for *"throw off"* implies in the original Greek excess body bulk! It may also refer to the heavy garments one wears that must be "thrown off" as one prepares to make the run. Everyone knows what extra baggage can do to a runner in a race! No serious runner would ever consider carrying around extra baggage when they are competing to win. This is the essence of "SELF DISCIPLINE" ... it is our responsibility before God to cast aside those things that become serious extra baggage, those things which might slow us down or sidetrack us. Self-discipline is needed to even get started!

The *"sin that so easily entangles us"* here is the sin of NO DISCIPLINE, or any sins that would prevent us from running or weigh us down! How easily sin strikes our lives! Without discipline there can be no success in a race! There has yet to be a world champion that never practiced! The Christian life doesn't just happen, it comes as the fruit of self-discipline along with God's graces.

Too much of the time we wait around for something spiritual to happen to our lives, when we should be preparing always for those spiritual things to take place in our lives. *A runner does not wait for the goal line to come to him, he goes to it!*

Hebrews 12:2-3

[2] fixing our eyes on Jesus, the pioneer and

perfecter of faith. For the joy set before him he endured the cross, scorning its shame, and sat down at the right hand of the throne of God. ³ Consider him who endured such opposition from sinners, so that you will not grow weary and lose heart.

"*Let us fix our eyes on Jesus...*" Here is where our focus should be! Good runners never look around them while they are running. This distracts them and causes them to lose their own pacing! Too often Christians do this today; we make decisions to drop out of this or that church, or this or that ministry based on someone else we are looking at. This is wrong! We are to be looking at Christ. He is the *"author"* (starting point) and *"finisher"* (goal line) of our faith, not other people! People can be examples (negative or positive), but not our focus!

Many times a runner will keep a single focus on something at the goal line to keep their path straight. Make sure you are fixing your eyes on the right source (Christ) or you might run crooked! Unlike the Olympics where you run to be the first place winner, running the race in spiritual terms is not to try to be first, but to be faithful and finish well!

Jesus becomes the perfect example for us to follow... He followed the course with joy even though it included pain and suffering because of the goal ... our salvation. It is amazing how much work Olympians go through for a single medal, often one they earned for just a few minutes of performance, but it took a lifetime of self-discipline to get there!

Hebrews 12:4-6

[4] In your struggle against sin, you have not yet resisted to the point of shedding your blood. [5] And have you completely forgotten this word of encouragement that addresses you as a father addresses his son? It says, "My son, do not make light of the Lord's discipline, and do not lose heart when he rebukes you, [6] because the Lord disciplines the one he loves, and he chastens everyone he accepts as his son."

These words were uttered by Scott Hamilton,

Olympic skater, shortly after winning his Gold medal: *"It was a moment to be shared. Someone asked me why I was looking at the medal so intently. What I was doing was looking at 16 years of my life."*

We are to consider the rewards that so far outstrip the sacrifices so that we do not become weary and lose heart! In all honesty there will be times you will feel like quitting. It will be tough to live a life of faith in a world that scoffs at it! Sometimes it is tough doing all the hard work and discipline when you see no results for it immediately, much like Olympians – they must keep fighting back the pain and losses with the idea that in the future the reward will come. Many runners have continued to compete with torn ligaments and injuries, very much in pain, but knowing the reward will be worth it in the end. Part of competition is pain and if we quit every time we hurt, we will never finish the course! Keep focused and faithful!

A good coach will use failures and pain to teach an athlete. God does at times bring discipline into our lives when we fail to use self-discipline. Nobody likes to preach on this subject, for it is not a pleasant idea! There are few "amens" when this comes up! However, even when God does bring discipline into our lives, it is never RETRIBUTION, it is REDEMPTIVE in focus!

The point of discipline is love, a love that cares too much to let someone learn self-destructive patterns. This is why parents discipline their children, to keep them from developing characteristics and qualities that ultimately will be destructive to a healthy and happy life. While it is hard to see them when you are on the side of being disciplined, the fruit of proper discipline shows itself later.

Hebrews 12:7-13

[7] Endure hardship as discipline; God is treating you as his children. For what children are not disciplined by their father? [8] If you are not disciplined—and everyone undergoes discipline—then you are not legitimate, not true sons and daughters at all. [9] Moreover, we have all had human fathers who disciplined us and we respected them for it. How much more should we submit to the

Father of spirits and live! ¹⁰ *They disciplined us for a little while as they thought best; but God disciplines us for our good, in order that we may share in his holiness.* ¹¹ *No discipline seems pleasant at the time, but painful. Later on, however, it produces a harvest of righteousness and peace for those who have been trained by it.*
¹² *Therefore, strengthen your feeble arms and weak knees.* ¹³ *"Make level paths for your feet," so that the lame may not be disabled, but rather healed.*

Rather than getting angry with God when He does allow discipline in our lives we should be grateful. God is using it to teach us to be self-disciplined and to correct our harmful patterns. With this knowledge we should then receive that discipline rather than run from it. Too many Christians fail to learn and thus are doomed to keep repeating the same mistakes over and over again! Too often we try and get as far away from the punishment as possible rather than approach it so we can learn from it and move on. Yet, to move closer to it is to move on quicker with less pain. To move away from it is to increase the pain and minimize the learning.

If we can accept our earthly father's discipline as an act of love, and respect them for caring enough to challenge us when we are wrong, how much more should we accept our Heavenly Father's discipline which is always perfect and from perfect love?

The whole purpose of this discipline is the fruit it will bear in our lives! As every child can testify, no punishment at the time seems pleasant when it happens, but later in our lives it will bear great fruit. God's discipline in this way is always redemptive! *It really did hurt Him more than it hurts us!* His son Jesus died on a cross to cover those failures of ours. In bearing our punishment, He has made possible our salvation!

God always disciplines us with this in mind, to return us to a fruitful life and not a fruitless one! The harvest is righteousness and peace! Discipline is part of our training! We can avoid His discipline if we practice correct self-discipline in many cases.

This same idea is found in the Gospels when

Jesus talks about *"pruning the branches"* in order to make them more fruitful. The *"we are the branches, He is the vine"* passage in John 15:4-6 – it is painful but productive.

The writer returns again to the training of an athlete image and encourages the listeners to *"strengthen your feeble arms and weak knees."* In other words, to deal with the weak areas in our lives! Failure to do this will cause us to stumble in the race which will lead to serious injury. It may also cause others to stumble that are running near us! Part of the plea here is to encourage their example in the face of a society that will surely be watching and who could easily stumble over those who fall! We have witnessed this in past years with well-known evangelists and pastors who have fallen through weaknesses and sins! Others have stumbled over their examples and thus kept some from the race! The world is watching; we must run strong for others to run well too. It is not just the responsibility of well-known Christians to run well for society's benefit, we all must run well for society to see that Christianity is real! It is a call to all of us to bear the responsibility!

There are a lot of Christians who are doing nothing. But there are no Christians who have nothing to do. – *Anonymous*

We cannot afford for the world to see "feeble" Christians. We need to be strong. The authenticity of the Gospel is at stake!

This final verse clinches the thought in verse 12 about our example in society and in the church: We are to make *"level paths for our feet so that the lame may not be disabled, but rather healed."* The word for *"LAME"* here literally means, "THOSE WHO WAVER BACK AND FORTH" a reference to those who are uncertain and uncommitted. Our path should be level so that our run is without obstacles that we could trip over – this would only cause those who are uncertain or uncommitted to ignore the path we are taking!

We bear a responsibility to keep a level path for our feet and for society! The Gospel is quite simple and pure, we must be careful not to clutter it up either by going off deep ends or by trying to make it so complicated that no one could understand it! We must not follow the crowd; rather we must lead and keep our own path clear!

Discipline, self or God's, is designed to help make our path level so we can lead society toward the cross of Christ. We are in a race! How well are you running?

The pursuit of spiritual maturity requires effort and focus in our lives. It is possible to get saved and not grow. We must, like all good athletes, learn to be responsible for our own growth in the Lord. No athlete succeeds without discipline and focus, and no believer will succeed without this either. How well are you running?

I am always amazed at the athletes during the winter and summer Olympics. I am amazed because they have perfected their bodies to push the envelope of human endurance to set new world records and to be the best in the world in their particular sport.

How do they get there? I have exercised at times, run a little here and a little there, but there is no way I could run in a race with those guys and gals. They got there by constant and persistent training. They have to learn to persevere through pain, through hardships, through long hours of training, and only then can they even begin to think of competing for the highest honor among athletic endeavors. If you want to be the best, you must persevere!

It is precisely this concept that the writer of Hebrews has in mind in this one kick-off verse to chapter 12. In fact, it is likely the writer has in mind the Olympics which were a reality back in his own day. The verse starts by talking about a great crowd of witnesses, like at an Olympic event, and the discipline training that an Olympic athlete would have to endure to achieve his or her goal. He is specific in his use of analogy here to those who ran races.

As in our own day of the Olympics, races were set up and the course decided by the Olympic committee. All the runner had to do was run the race marked out faster and better than any other runner to win the gold. The writer of Hebrews likens this to the race God has marked out for each of us and encourages us to run it with perseverance.

The Bible teaches us that God has established a

course and race for every one of His followers. To achieve what He has in mind for our lives we will need to run with perseverance, even when it gets tough in life.

With the writer of Hebrews use of running a race he is clearly indicating that life will at times be difficult and challenging – all races were in the Olympics. There has never been an "easy" race in world competition. Living the life of faith is going to be tough at times! Like any Olympic runner, there are days when you simply have to push through to stay in the game. Yes, it can be hard to be a Christian, but it is also going to be worth the crown at the end.

The context of chapter 11 included a long list of names of God's people who were delivered from difficulties, AND some who were not, but still had faith. This is the challenge of living by faith, that sometimes we have to have the discipline to believe and trust God when things don't work out like we would like. And, in such tough times we have to have the discipline when this happens of continuing to press on in our walk with God, trusting in the ultimate prize. The athlete who competed sometimes had painful experiences and setbacks during the race, but the only thing they had in mind when these things happened was the goal line! As God's people we will at times encounter setbacks, painful experiences that would otherwise take us out of the race, but the true athlete just doesn't stop. He/she perseveres through the pain with the goal line in mind, and the ultimate prize. The only way to do this is to simply persevere, to keep going. Notice that is precisely what the writer in Hebrews 12:1b states, *"...let us run with perseverance the race marked out for us."* To do that requires a stubborn but positive discipline.

Runners understand that there is a place during a long race when you have to push through the pain to catch a second wind. There is a place while running where you simply want to quit, and your body screams in pain and says, "Enough already!" It is at this point that all the discipline of preparation and perseverance in training has to kick in order to finish and win! Ironically, when the running hits this *"wall"* of pain and does not stop, the body kicks into another mode and catches what is known as the *"second wind."* When your body realizes that all its screaming won't stop your run, it reorganizes to burn other kinds of energy in order to give you the final push. Sometimes this includes the release of hormones in the brain called endorphins which actually give the runner a sense of exuberance and a sense of wellbeing – it is the body's natural way of controlling pain. Endorphins are natural narcotics that help diminish the pain. There are similar spiritual parallels to this. Sometimes in our race in life we hit tough places. It is then when all the spiritual disciplines in our lives kick in and help us find God's peace even when circumstances would dictate contrary wise. There is a *"peace that passes understanding"* – our spiritual endorphins that allow us to press through in painful times. (Phil. 4:7)

When everything says *"stop"* our perseverance says, *"Keep going!"* There are times when you would like to quit! Pain is always the natural way to get us to stop something. But a true athlete knows that pain has to be evaluated and if it is just the pain from the run and not some broken part, you have to simply use determination or perseverance to push through the pain to victory. We must learn this as God's people too! The writer is indicating that God has a race for each one of us. In order to achieve the goal line we will have times we will have to push through the pain and trust the strength of God to get us to the finish line where the prize awaits us.

World class athletes are determined people. World class believers are too! God help us as His people to show the world that we are not quitters, that we will endure the race with perseverance and show others what the power of faith can do!

This world does everything it can to live easy, and our bodies today tell the story of a life that is so sedentary that our bodies could hardly endure a small trial of pain. I wonder if this is true in many of our churches as well. A little pain and many believers are ready to quit. They no longer feel they can trust God who has disappointed their expectations. The problem may be the false expectations! There is not a world class runner on this planet that assumes running their race is going to be without difficulties or pain! But they are not focused on the pain or difficulties! They are focused on the prize! And if an earthly medal of gold, or a wreath as it was in the first century, was enough to make them endure through endless hours of pain and struggle, how much more for us who know that at the finish line there awaits us the crown of life for eternity with God! This life is not just about getting more stuff, more money, more ease, it is about running the race that God has marked out for us and not quitting, about persevering to the very end! This is what the writer in Hebrews is trying to convey. If earthly runners will discipline and endure their race for a simple wreath, or even a gold medal today – how much more should we endure for the crown of life? We need believers today that simply don't quit! We need believers today who will persevere through the trials of pain and setbacks, to keep running and running well to the very end.

God has marked out a race for each one of us. We all have a destiny to fulfill. Notice his statement: *"...let us run with perseverance THE RACE MARKED OUT FOR US."* We are not just stumbling through life with no road to follow. God has for each one of us a race to endure, a path to follow, a destiny to fulfill. We are here with purpose in this life. We will have to discover the path He has created for us to fulfill, and then pursue that with all our hearts. We can stray off course if we are not obedient to the one who has set that path for us! A runner listens to his coach – the coach knows the best route and the proper pacing for the runner. If for some reason the runner chooses not to obey his/her coach he invites possible defeat in his run. God has given us the path – it is in His Word. Obedience to the Word of God is the best way to ensure that we stay on the path of righteousness, which is the path that brings us to the finish line.

Jesus declared that He Himself is the PATH. Jesus said, *"I am the way, the truth, and the life: no man comes to the Father, but by me."* (John 14:6) The only path God has ordained for men to follow is Jesus Himself!

All other roads lead away from the finish line where awaits the prize. Tragically, there will be many who will run their own race throughout their lifetime and fail to arrive at the proper finish line. It was a tragic thing when a runner went off the proper path and had to be disqualified from the race – any other race except the one God has laid out for us all will lead to failure.

It is truly sad when world class runners who had run so well their race discovered at the end that they had taken a wrong turn somewhere and because of that were disqualified by the officials and removed from becoming a winner. It wouldn't matter that they finished first. If they took a wrong turn on the course, they still would be disqualified for failing to stay on the proper course!

The whole point of running with perseverance is to WIN! Yes, there actually is a destination for living our lives. It is not just about having a good time during this lifetime, although that is not wrong in and of itself.

There is a real point to living and living correctly. The person who refuses to believe in God or eternity simply has no other destination in life than to please themselves. Thus it shouldn't surprise us that the goals for those who don't know Christ are self-centered, or simply are geared toward finding happiness instead of finding holiness. Yet, at the end of their lives there will be no point to having lived if they don't realize that this life is all preparation for the next. Someone once said, *"If you don't want God in your life here, do not expect to have Him in your life there!"*

What are you living for?

Actually, the disciplines in your life will tell that story! What you strive for ultimately is what you believe in. A runner can truly believe they are winning the race while they are running, but tragically discover at the end that they lose because they ran the wrong race or ran on the wrong path! In such cases the sadness is profound, because they ran hard, they were disciplined, they pushed through difficulties, but only at the end discovered they were disqualified for failure to run the right race! But oh the joy when we discover at the end that all the pain we pushed through, all the disciplines during life, all the training we endured pays off at the end and the crown of life is given to us! A crown that never fades away like the old wreaths given during the Olympics in antiquity, or even the gold medals given today. There will come a day when gold will mean nothing.

It will all be worth it one day. We just need to stay on course, push through the times of pain, trust the disciplines of spiritual exercises, and trust the path (Jesus) Who has guaranteed the race will be won! The destination is eternity with God, and joy forever more.

Will it be worth all the spiritual exercises at the end of life, will it be worth pushing through all the painful events in life, the discouragement of struggles, the difficulties of hard work to stay on the path of righteousness? You better believe it will be worth it all! Christ has marked out a race for each one of us, and when we run with perseverance we will discover at the end of the race the crown of victory, the crown of life, and joy for evermore with God Himself.

As the old chorus, *It Will Be Worth It All,* by Esther Kerr Rusthoi states, seeing Jesus will be our reward. We won't regret the trials of this life once we get a glimpse of His face. In that moment, all our sorrow will be wiped away.

WHAT'S YOUR DESTINATION IN LIFE?

Power in Thanksgiving!

Hebrews 12:28-29

This invitation is pregnant with powerful thanksgiving! It is a call to be thankful AND worship God, for He alone has an eternal Kingdom and He is forever the eternal King! When we live thankful it affects others as well as ourselves!

With this in mind the writer of Hebrews is communicating that the believer can be in a state of joy and thanksgiving even when the worst of things seem to be happening around them. Our identity and future are not hinged on what this temporary world is able to provide. It is not based on the hope of things here and now. Our thankfulness and worship are possible because of a truth that God will supplant anything this world now knows – we are members of a Kingdom that cannot fail, and a King that will not be overthrown!

So, we can be thankful and worship God in the very midst of a nightmare reality on this planet! Our praise to God is not based on this current world and its hopes. Our praise to God is based on the fact that His kingdom is never failing, and our King will never fail – and that we are members of that Kingdom forever! We have a guaranteed future!

The Bible teaches us that our stability, our joy, our hope is based on a reality greater than this current world with all its empires and promises! Our hope is a blessed hope on being members of a Kingdom that will never fail, and a King that will rule triumphantly forever!

In Hebrews 12:28a, the word *"Therefore..."* introduces the conclusions to follow. It is a safe conclusion drawn by the facts that the God who worked in the Old Covenant has a better promise in mind in the New Covenant. *"Since we are receiving..."* – here the writer is referencing something real, and something already happening that will continue to unfold. The good news here is that we are already benefiting from the future – we are already receiving a more permanent Kingdom! Sinners always have their pasts catching up to them! Believers always have their futures catching up to them! No wonder the writer can talk about giving thanks and worship to God – the future is secure for those who are members of His kingdom! Even if things here and now are not so good, if kingdoms here are collapsing and failing, we have a solid future! We need to live in such a way that others see that we believe in tomorrow, that there is more to come!

Hebrews 12:28-29

[28] Therefore, since we are receiving a kingdom that cannot be shaken, let us be thankful, and so worship God acceptably with reverence and awe, [29] for our "God is a consuming fire."

God has promised His people a permanent future kingdom! And in real ways we are already receiving it. So many things in this world are temporary, but not His kingdom! Even great nations collapse in time, and kings have to be replaced, but

Jesus' kingdom and His rule will have no end! Our future is secure!

No current or future power will cause its collapse. Abraham and others journeyed through this life and its difficulties knowing that there was a better city, a better country coming. This hope has been the basis for saints of all time to endure whatever suffering this world has caused. We are on unshakeable ground in His kingdom!

Everything prior had only been shadows of greater realities, even Israel's old kingdom and all its glory. God has always had something better in mind for His people. Even Abraham understood this truth: *"For he was looking forward to the city with foundations, whose architect and builder is God."* (Heb. 11:10) Others also grasped this more permanent promise: *"You sympathized with those in prison and joyfully accepted the confiscation of your property, because you knew that you yourselves had better and lasting possessions."* (Heb. 10:34) Because of this truth of a future and a more permanent kingdom the writer to the Hebrews wrote this earlier: *"So do not throw away your confidence; it will be richly rewarded."* (Heb. 10:35)

It is precisely this truth that enabled the early saints, even those under the Old Covenant, to endure unbelievable things. They were never focused only on the here and now! How many of us have forgotten the importance of believing in this "Blessed Hope" of Jesus' coming again, and of a kingdom that will never fade or pass away? *The measure of our confidence in God's promise of the future will determine the measure of our ability to endure the present difficulties.* Every time Israel lost sight of God's future promises they wanted to go back, and they complained. What about us, do we get angry with God for the current conditions of this life, do we feel cheated, etc.? If our confidence and hope is NOT on this stuff here and now our faith cannot be shaken, because as the writer says in our text, *"We are receiving a kingdom that cannot be shaken…"* (Heb. 12:28a). This is all meant to be much more than a theological or theoretical truth, it is meant to be the foundation of our hope, our worship, and our trust in God.

The confidence of this permanent Kingdom and King should provoke a response from those who belong to it, and it is stated in Hebrews 12:28b, *"Let us be thankful, and so worship God acceptably with reverence and awe."* While we face this world we never face it alone! And God should always be the focal point for the direction of our life! Remember, it is the King in Heaven that is our focus, not the kings or kingdoms of this earth!

Failure to be thankful and worship God is a good indicator that we have not taken seriously these future realities and promises. Either we don't believe them truly ... or we are not reflecting on them and grasping them correctly. Thankfulness and worship should be the *"natural"* outflow from a heart that is confident about the privilege of being sons and daughters of the Most High God! To all of us who belong to this permanent kingdom – we are a privileged people! There is no greater privilege than being part of God's unending kingdom! People of privilege usually rejoice over their exalted status. How about us?

Great promise, great permanence, great privilege leads to great PRAISE! This is the idea of the word *"acceptably"* in the text! Acceptable worship is praise. 1 Peter 2:9 states, *"But you are a chosen people, a royal priesthood, a holy nation, a people belonging to God, that you may declare the praises of him who called you out of darkness into his wonderful light."* When we are given a great gift, it is natural to express praise! Therefore when we are not praising God we have lost sight of the great gifts and promises that are ours! Praise should be natural for the believer.

This final verse at first appears out of context to the previous one, but it not! *"For our 'God is a consuming fire.'"* What was the writer's point amidst all the joy and praise at saying this? It was akin to saying, *"God is all powerful!"* This was a throwback reference to the Old Covenant when Israel came to the mountain and was fearful of God's presence. There was lightning, thunder, and fire … they were scared! Under the Old Covenant they pulled back out of fear. God's power was overwhelming to them! But under the New Covenant we need NOT be afraid, in fact – it is His power that guarantees the future! We serve a King that shall never be dethroned! We serve a King that we can approach without fear! It is important to understand that God is all powerful! Yet, Jesus' conquering death proved that nothing can collapse God's power!

How else can we have confidence in the future? God is a consuming fire in the sense that there is nothing that is greater than Him! It wasn't meant here as a negative, but to inspire reverence and awe! The New Testament saint can come boldly into His presence, with reverence and awe, and praise and worship! However, for the unbeliever, God's presence may still inspire fear! The invitation is for us to "come." We stand on the promise assured that there is a permanent Kingdom! And we stand on the promise that we have an everlasting King – *"Let us be thankful and worship!"*

The promise is a great one. No matter what the kingdoms of this world do, how many of them collapse, how many kings rule over them – our future is not dependent on these current kingdoms and kings! Our hope is built on the sure promise of a kingdom that will never end, and a King that will never cease from ruling! And, for all those who know Him, who have believed in Him, we will forever rule and reign with Him. *"Therefore, since we are receiving a kingdom that cannot be shaken, let us be thankful, and so worship God acceptably with reverence and awe."* (Heb. 12:28) Amen!

Christ, the Only Way

Hebrews 13:11-14

The early Christians who had been Jewish struggled to accept the power of Christ's sacrifice for their sins! There was a tendency once saved to go back to those things which they once held dear as practices, things that in truth were only shadows of the greater substance found in Christ. It can be amazing the kinds of old laws man will keep just to feel "secure" and have life be predictable. Yet, these old laws can be meaningless today even if they served a purpose before.

Hebrews 13:11-14

[11] The high priest carries the blood of animals

> *into the Most Holy Place as a sin offering, but the bodies are burned outside the camp.*
> *^{12} And so Jesus also suffered outside the city gate to make the people holy through his own blood. ^{13} Let us, then, go to him outside the camp, bearing the disgrace he bore. ^{14} For here we do not have an enduring city, but we are looking for the city that is to come.*

We can follow a similar path once we embrace Christ as our Lord. If we are not careful we can begin the process of "adding" lots of other conditions for salvation as time progresses. Sometimes these "things" can be very helpful truths pertaining to living a life of faith, but they can grow beyond that to a type of legalism that demands others practice all these "other things" in order to be saved!

When this happens the Gospel starts to look like a list of do's and don'ts – even though some of those things should be a part of the life of a believer, they must not become conditions in order to be saved. There is nothing more to add to the fact that Jesus died for all our sins, and accepting

Him is the only basis for salvation! The "living out" of faith is the practice of "sanctification" – the life of holiness that grows in the life of the believer.

The Bible teaches us that Christ is the only way of salvation! It is not the laws we hold to that are created to make us look "holy" to others. It is not the expectations that religious people have … the only way to God is through faith in the sacrifice of Christ on Calvary, His shed blood and resurrection!

The Old Covenant was a bloody one! Because of man's constant sinful behaviors it was necessary to have frequent blood sacrifices for their forgiveness. Just imagine what life was like! Constant sacrifices, with many animals killed to shed blood for the remission of sins. It was a constant reminder of just how difficult it was to live for God. Each animal killed was another reminder of the terrible price of sin, and the need for it to be cleansed. How visible is the evidence of sin's cost? Innocent animals had to shed their blood for man to not have his own blood shed. There was a terrible price tag for sin! All these of course were but shadows of the ultimate lamb of God that would be slain to take away the sins of the world once and for all. The shadows were bad enough, but the ultimate sacrifice of Jesus on the cross of Calvary and the shedding of His blood was horrific! Looking back would only slow them down; they needed to be looking forward to home to move along!

Yet, without the shedding of blood there was no remission of sin! Even in Eden, after the first sin – Adam and Eve were hiding from God, ashamed and exposed (naked). In their own efforts to cover their shame of nakedness they covered themselves with fig leaves. However, this didn't appear to cover the shame. They were still hiding from God after they covered their nakedness! Instead, God comes and takes the skin of animals and clothes them – this very act required that He kill animals and shed their blood to gain the skins that were used to clothe Adam and Eve. Thus, Adam and Eve witnessed the first blood sacrifice to cover their sinfulness – a sacrifice done by God Himself, but only a shadow of the ultimate "Lamb of God" which would be the final sacrifice. Thousands of years passed with the constant need to shed blood under the Old Covenant.

These sacrifices and blood had to be carried into

the Holy Place by dedicated priests, who in turn would burn the bodies of the animals outside the camp. Nothing was saved or used for food in these sacrifices for sin. The people only felt secure once the ceremony had been complete. And the people had to rely on these priests to perform the duties for them; they could not provide the service themselves. Their security lay at the feet of leaders who would do the right thing. And yet, even a careful adherence to the letter of the law could ultimately not save anyone. It all depended on the Messiah who would come and fulfill the law and the Spirit of the Law and lay His life down for us. The letter of the law would only kill.

This was a precarious position to be in. What if their leaders were corrupt, what happened to their sins if there was failure by the priests? Indeed the Old Testament is full of poor examples, even some priests whom God killed because of their wickedness and improper leadership. No man could come before God in the Holy Place without being the right clan and the right kind of priest. However, in the New Covenant we have a high priest, Jesus, who has opened up the Holy of Holies for us all to enter, covered by the blood of the Lamb of God, so we are cleansed and can come individually! The day Jesus died on the cross the Bible says that there was a terrible earthquake that tore the curtain before the Holy of Holies in the Temple in half, thus opening up the way for anyone to enter – Jesus opened the way! And as the author of Hebrews says here, Jesus matched that Old Covenant shadow by not only shedding His blood as God's lamb, but by dying outside the camp, or the walls of Jerusalem. The writer was clearly identifying Jesus as the ultimate sacrifice that fulfills all the shadows of the Old Covenant in full!

Jesus is the final and ultimate sacrifice for man's sins! Jesus became the substance of the shadow in the Old Covenant. No longer is there a need for constant blood sacrifices for sins. Jesus' death on Calvary which took place outside the city gates is the final and full sacrifice for all time. There is no other place we can go to find cleansing from our sins. Only through Christ and His shed blood have all the shadows in the Old Covenant ceremonies been fulfilled. Any man-made attempt at cleansing would have ruined us!

Christ carried the entire burden for sins. He is the *"Lamb of God which takes away the sin of the world"* as John the Baptist declared in John 1:29 (NIV): *"The next day John saw Jesus coming toward him and said, 'Look, the Lamb of God, who takes away the sin of the world!'"* It does require us to accept this gift for it to be applied. How tragic that such a gift is available but not accepted. Even in the Old Covenant, the person who wanted their sins forgiven had to accept the blood sacrifice for their sins.

Christ has made the way possible, though He died outside the gates of the city, although He was an outcast of the Jews and their sacrificial system. Their failure to see that Jesus was the substance to the shadows of the Old meant that they remained in their sins. Refusal to accept the proper sacrifice meant refusal to be forgiven.

What about us today? We too must be willing to accept this once-and-for-all sacrifice of Christ's in order to experience His cleansing power. Why would anyone prefer the shadows over substance? Through Christ's own blood which He shed, we are able to be cleansed. No wonder the writer in

Hebrews here said, *"Let us, then, go to Him outside the camp, bearing the disgrace He bore."* Do not throw away such a great invitation, such a great salvation! The idea of *"going outside the camp"* is to leave behind all the systems and religions of the past or future and go directly to Christ as the perfect sacrifice. Nothing created or made by man will satisfy a Holy God. Man who is a sinner by nature cannot please or satisfy a Holy God – so we must go *"outside the camp"* to find the acceptable sacrifice that will allow us to be accepted by a Holy God, and only Christ's shed blood as the perfect sinless Lamb of God can provide that. There is no other way to God! We need to pick the way out, not the old ways we knew – they will lead to death, but the path out through Jesus leads to life.

The emphasis on the first part of Hebrews 13:13 is, *"LET US, THEN, GO…"* The responsibility at this point is for us to make the move toward God! While Christ has made the way open, it is still up to us to come to Him! This means it is possible to NOT COME. The start of this verse is one of invitation, one of asking for response. The request is for others to join and go along.

For all those who actually go *"outside the camp"* and discover the sacrifice for sins in Christ, not only is there joy in the forgiveness of sins – there is a future city that will endure forever.

Today we can guarantee a future by accepting the blood sacrifice of Jesus Christ. Our hope for the future is dependent on what we do today, and about what Christ did yesterday!

This invitation of "LET US" is to find the cleansing from all sin that is needed. It is an invitation to provide for the future joy and happiness that God intended for man to have. It is however just that, an invitation – one that has to be responded to. In order for the blood of the sacrifice to cleanse, one has to apply the blood to the agent to be saved. Failure to do this means no cleansing. So, how can we neglect so great a salvation? *"Let us, then, go..."*

More than Lip Service

Hebrews 13:15-16
Romans 12:1-2

Mention the word "Worship" to someone and see how they respond! To most people the idea of "Worship" is something that happens on a Sunday morning in a building somewhere called a church. For some, the conditions have to be just perfect in order for them to worship – too often people don't enjoy worship unless things are just right, thus we are good at finding all kinds of reasons to avoid church! Imagine the world acting like this!

Worship and praise are not something that comes just from the right conditions around us, it comes from the heart and from our life. We are always worshipping, it is not just what happens on

Sunday morning!

The Bible will teach us that both our LIPS and our LIFE should be offering up praise to God continuously.

Hebrews 13:15-16

^{15} Through Jesus, therefore, let us continually offer to God a sacrifice of praise—the fruit of lips that openly profess his name. ^{16} And do not forget to do good and to share with others, for with such sacrifices God is pleased.

Notice in the text the link that makes this new communication possible: *"Through Jesus..."* Praise and worship cannot happen without coming through Christ! Praise is not just something we do, it is what we are and who we are connected to; and being connected to Christ is what makes praise even possible! Notice here also the sense of praise being *"continual!"* It is not just at church where praise from our lips is supposed to happen! The reason it is called a *"sacrifice of praise"* is because it won't always be convenient or when we simply feel like it!

There is a real sense here that how we communicate all the time is a part of worship. Every word from our lips should be *"praise"* in some form or fashion to God reflecting Christ in our lives. Our lips should confess praise and gratitude at all times reflecting Christ's reality in our lives!

It is our language at home, work, and church that is in view in the passage, that our lips are offering up to God *"CONTINUALLY"* a sacrifice of praise! How should this impact the way we talk about others? How should this impact the jokes we tell co-workers on the job? How should this impact our speech around home and family? As well as how we enter into the service at church! Too often it is far easier to express praise in a worship service than it is in day-to-day routines, yet the sense of *"continuously"* and *"sacrifice"* here indicate the daily routine as well as the church service.

It is clear that what we say comes from how we think, hence how this passage fits well with the *"fruit of lips"* issue in Hebrews 13:15! We speak how we think! (Luke 6:45: *"out of the heart the mouth speaks"*) If we are to offer up a sacrifice of praise as the *"fruit of our lips"* on an ongoing basis, it will have to spring from the way we think in our hearts and minds! Paul writes here to express the importance of *"conformity"* – but to be cautious not to conform any longer to the thinking of this world! The world has little concern for worship and praise of God and if we allow the world's influence to infiltrate our entire thinking processes we will find our sense of worship distorted as well! The world puts little value on verbal expressions to God. It is a low priority if one at all! We must be careful that the emphasis of the world does not become ours! (See Phil. 4:8-9 – *We are to think on the right things, not part of the natural man.*)

The problem for many Christians today is that we have too compartmentalized our lives into chunks. We think of worship as only this *"chunk"* of time spent in a church building on Sunday a.m. and don't see how worship is a part of the rest of our week or our activities! We should develop a *"worship"* mentality in everything! We would be completely different as people if we really had a *"KINGDOM OF GOD"* mentality over everything in our daily lives and not just when we are in a church building! In the strictest sense everything we do is a part of worshipping God, and all our daily mundane things in life are a part of that expression!

Think about how the emphasis in our lives would be changed if we really thought this way. Everything we say and everything we do tests and approves the will of God – hopefully our lips and our actions will show *"His good, pleasing and perfect will!"* The idea here is to have our minds transformed by God's Word so that we are no longer conformed to this world and its way of thinking! The Greek word translated here *"transform"* is *"metamorpho"* from which we get our English word *"metamorphosis."* The idea is that we change from the way the world thinks to the way God thinks, a process of becoming something new and different! This is no doubt a process – worship always is! The renewing of our minds will enable us to think very differently from this world, and by thinking differently we will speak differently! This will enable us to have the fruit of our lips worship God continuously!

As soon as the writer of Hebrews talks about the *"fruit of lips"* as a sacrifice of praise he moves to his next thought tying this together with *"do not forget to do good and to share with others, for with such sacrifices God is pleased."* The *"fruit of lips"* results in the *"fruit of living"* and vice versa! <u>What we SPEAK we tend to SHOW</u>! *(Remember in school "SHOW & TELL")* and what we SHOW we tend to SPEAK! What we do as good to others is also a part of our worship of God. It will bear fruit at some point in our lives as well as theirs!

The world does not just look at what we *"say"* but also what we *"do"* in determining what kind of *"worshipper"* we are! The world will rarely criticize our <u>worship style</u> if they know our <u>lifestyle</u> is also godly! We show people what a *"sacrifice of praise"* is not just by the way we verbally worship on Sunday mornings, but how we live Monday through Saturday! God is pleased with our *"sacrifices of praise"* when they come from both our LIPS and our LIVES! The idea from God's standpoint is that our LIPS match our LIVES! Since this *"sacrifice of praise"* is supposed to be *"continuous"* it is supposed to be a constant flow from both our lips in a *"worship"* service, and from our lives in *"willful"* service!

Here Paul picks up this very theme. To worship means to give up more than a couple of hours on

Sunday a.m. to offer worship as *LIP SERVICE*. It means to offer up our own bodies as a *LIVING SACRIFICE!* To offer up our bodies as a *"living sacrifice"* is *"pleasing"* to God! The only problem with a *"living sacrifice"* is that it has a tendency to *"crawl off the altar when the fire gets hot under it!"* This really means that God should get the best of us! For too many Christians, Christianity is like a weekend thing you do, and so it is treated like *"going to the movies"* or going somewhere else. It doesn't have the commitment of the best from us all the time. Only western Christianity has this concept of compartmentalizing our relationship to God! Many other religions see their commitment to their gods as all embracing; their gods always get their best, not their leftover time and resources!

Can we say that God gets our very best, or just whatever we have leftover in time, resources, and priorities? It is always too easy to see a sacrifice as something we give, or even something we do, but we need to see the sacrifice as OURSELVES! – a living one! Paul says that such a living sacrifice in view of God's mercy is a *"SPIRITUAL ACT OF WORSHIP!"* The word *"spiritual"* here in Greek is

"LOGIKOS" from where we get our word *"LOGICAL."* In view of God's mercy it is only LOGICAL that we offer up our bodies as a living sacrifice for God to use! This is both *"reasonable"* (KJV) and *"logical!"* Why would God want just the worship of our lips without the worship from our lives?

If we are to offer up *"sacrifices of praise"* we must be willing to offer up our lives as living sacrifices. This will then include what comes from our lips! When done out of love, this sacrifice will not be viewed as a LOSS, but as GAIN!

Too often we think of *"sacrifice"* as a painful loss, but in reality it is a joyous thing – *"holy and pleasing to God."* To God, the content of our worship is wrapped up in the character of the worshipper! The real life of *"worship"* then is both what comes from our *"LIPS"* and from our *"LIVES!"* So did you come this morning *"to worship"* or as *"a worshipper?"* Are you *"continuously offering up to God a sacrifice of praise"* or just when you are in the *"service?"*

Are both your LIPS and your LIFE engaged in praising God?

"LET US OFFER UP SACRIFICES OF PRAISE!"

Romans 12:1-2

¹ Therefore, I urge you, brothers and sisters, in view of God's mercy, to offer your bodies as a living sacrifice, holy and pleasing to God—this is your true and proper worship. ² Do not conform to the pattern of this world, but be transformed by the renewing of your mind. Then you will be able to test and approve what God's will is—his good, pleasing and perfect will.

The concept of *"praising God"* is far more reaching than just what happens on a Sunday morning worship service! It is also far more reaching than a song of praise or two! The crowds on Palm Sunday were quick to praise Christ with their lips, but not with their lives! Praise is a lifestyle of glorifying Christ and not just lips that gush, *"Glory to God in the highest!"*

Did you come TO worship, or did you come AS a worshipper? Let us offer up sacrifices of praise through our lips and our lives!

About Tim R. Barker

Reverend Tim R. Barker is the Superintendent of the South Texas District of the Assemblies of God which is headquartered in Houston, Texas

He is a graduate of Southwestern Assemblies of God University, with a Bachelor of Science degree in General Ministries /Biblical Studies, with a minor in music. He also received a Master of Arts in Practical Theology from SAGU and received his Doctorate of Ministry Degree from West Coast Seminary.

Reverend Barker was ordained by the Assemblies of God in 1989. He began his ministry in the South Texas District in 1984 as youth & music minister and continued his ministry as Pastor, Executive Presbyter (2006 – 2009) and Executive Secretary-Treasurer (2009 – 2011) in the South Texas District, where he served until his election as the South Texas District Superintendent in 2011.

By virtue of his district office, Reverend Barker is a member of the District's Executive Presbytery and the General Presbytery of the General Council of the Assemblies of God, Springfield, Missouri. He is a member of the Executive Board of Regents for Southwestern Assemblies of God University, Waxahachie, Texas and SAGU-American Indian College, Phoenix, Arizona. He is a member of the Board of Directors of Pleasant Hills Children's Home, Fairfield, Texas, as well as numerous other boards and committees.

Reverend Barker and his wife, Jill, married in 1983, have been blessed with two daughters. Jordin and her husband, Stancle Williams, who serves as the South Texas District Youth Director. Abrielle and her husband, Nolan McLaughlin are church planters of Motion Church in San Antonio. The Barkers have four grandchildren, Braylen, Emory and Landon Williams and Kingston McLaughlin.

His unique style of pulpit ministry and musical background challenges the body of Christ, with an appeal that reaches the generations.

A Final Word

You can find Tim on the South Texas District website at www.stxag.org, on Facebook, or at his Houston office when he's not traveling his home state ministering in the churches across the South Texas District.

He'd be thrilled to connect with you and share stories of God's faithfulness.

www.ingramcontent.com/pod-product-compliance
Lightning Source LLC
Chambersburg PA
CBHW071123090426
42736CB00012B/1987